Dentists,
Hygienists,
and Cows

Advance Praise for
Dentists, Hygientists, and Cows

"*Dentists, Hygienists, and Cows* by Brandi Hooker Evans offers an innovative perspective on dental care, advocating for personalized, compassionate treatment strategies. The book is enriched with humor, notably through Evans's own experiences, making complex dental topics approachable and engaging. It's a compelling read for dental professionals seeking to enhance their practice through effective, proven methods, promising not only healthier patients and a more enjoyable work environment but also a profitable business. This blend of clinical excellence and levity makes it a must-read for those in the dental field looking to invigorate their approach to patient care."

—**Penny Reed**, Chief Growth Officer, eAssist Dental Solutions, Author of *Growing Your Dental Business* and *Persuade With A Case Acceptance Story*

"*Dentists, Hygienists, and Cows* by Brandi Hooker is an invigorating read designed to rejuvenate the mindset of dental professionals. Through her extensive experience and passion for dentistry, Hooker Evans introduces innovative communication strategies to help professionals articulate the connection between oral health and overall well-being to their patients.

Dentists, Hygienists, and Cows empowers readers with the knowledge to inspire patients to take control of their health, offering valuable insights for both seasoned practitioners and newcomers to the field. It serves as a comprehensive guide equivalent to a week's worth of continuing education, promising to reignite the enthusiasm for patient care in the dental operatory."

—**Wendy Baxley**, RDH

"Brandi Hooker Evans' *Dentists, Hygienists, and Cows* breathes new life into a PROFESSION that has always been a source of spiritual and material gratification for practitioners and a fountain of wellness for those seeking their services. This book is a must-read for anyone who seeks not only to retain those rewards, but also to take the practice of Dentistry to a higher level. Written in language that's simple to understand with exercises that are easy to implement, *Dentists, Hygienists, and Cows* is pure genius. You can even feel Brandi's presence in the room when you read it! Get a copy for each member of your team and read it together. The result will be a happy and productive team that makes a difference for everyone they touch."

—**Alan G Stern**, DDS, Speaker, Coach,
Author of *Enjoy The Ride*

"Brand's love, light, and kindness shine through the pages of this book. I appreciate the co-diagnosing with patients, I do the same with myofunctional issues. I agree it helps them to understand so much more and get the buy in from their end."

—**Joy Lantz**, RDH

"Brandi Hooker Evans has created a fun, informative book that highlights her humorous style while providing dental teams with the knowledge to improve patients' lives and oral-systemic health. Breaking down the importance of all team members understanding how their interactions with patients can improve overall health, Brandi provides easily digestible information in a fun dialogue with the reader. Adding notes, thoughts, arguments, and to-dos at the end of each chapter reinforces the ideas presented and allows the reader to actively participate in improving oral-systemic health of the patients they treat."

—**Ann-Marie DePalma**, CDA, RDH, MEd

Dentists, Hygienists, AND Cows

How Brilliant
Dental Professionals
Have Great Days
While Providing Exquisite
Individualized Care

Brandi Hooker Evans, RDH-ER, MHE, MAADH

INDIE BOOKS
INTERNATIONAL

Dentists, Hygienists, and Cows

ISBN-13: 978-1-957651-72-9

Library of Congress Control Number: 2024905810

Cover photograph by Cami Ellis at Newborn Photography

Cows with ear tags and sunsets: Ryan Nelson of Rockland Valley Ranches

Individual cows: Tina Clinger of Clinger Farms

Designed by Melissa Farr

INDIE BOOKS INTERNATIONAL®, INC.
2511 WOODLANDS WAY
OCEANSIDE, CA 92054
www.indiebooksintl.com

This book is dedicated to every human who has ever gone into the healthcare profession to make a positive difference in this world.

While the information is heavy on dental geekery, the spirit applies across the healthcare board. 🥰

CONTENTS

Preface	Why Cows?	1
Chapter 1	It's All Greek To Me	9
Chapter 2	Donkeys And Dentistry	15
Chapter 3	Case Presentation (More Like Case Shushing)	29
Chapter 4	When They Ask You	35
Chapter 5	Whoa, Whoa, Whoa!	41
Chapter 6	Doing It For The Mooooo-lah?	49
Chapter 7	KISS	53
Chapter 8	Clean Up That Stinkin' Mess!	59
Chapter 9	"Whatever It Takes"	69
Chapter 10	Team, Team, T T T T T T Team, Team, Team	77
Chapter 11	The Freaking Finances	87
Chapter 11.2	Hope	95
Chapter 12	Care For The Whole, Not Just The Hole	103

Chapter 13   Abstinence   117

Chapter 14   Yeehaw!   121

Acknowledgments   123
About The Author   127

Appendix A – Auto Note Example   129
Appendix B – "How to" Spend the Appointment
                in Health   131
Appendix C – Radiograph Review   133
Appendix D – Endnotes   135

Why Cows?

Hi. I'm Brandi. I'm an Idaho gal through and through. I live in the east side of the state and grew up in the west. I drive back and forth frequently. Watching the farmland pass by is a view that comforts me all the way to my soul. Tractors and sprinklers that care for crops bring me joy and remind me *we reap what we sow.* Cows of all kinds seem to be enjoying the outdoors and unaware of human drama. They accept what is and live in the present. While they will get upset upon provocation, ruminating in anger and anxiety is not their method of operation. They are cared for most frequently as herds. Their individuality and emotional range are limited, not at all similar to a human, yet we dental professionals often approach patient care like we're herding cattle. Now is the perfect time for us to enjoy the farmer's ability to herd cattle and upgrade our delivery of care with the individuality needed to help the patients we love so dearly.

In dentistry, it goes like this: adults get an hour for a prophylaxis, radiographs, an exam, and fluoride. The patients attend a hygiene appointment. We proceed to do everything we can to fit them into that "one-hour prophy" stall. This herding technique is hurting our patients. In addition, the insurance companies are akin to villainous cowboys. It is as though we dentists and hygienists are the fearful townspeople, allowing them to ride in on their black horses and dictate how dental care will go. This corrupt cycle is decades old, and I propose we leave all of it behind. Put it out to pasture where it belongs.

At the time of this writing, in 2023, 3.5 billion people live on this earth with oral disease. Roughly half of everyone everywhere is struggling with oral infection. Many are unaware. What's worse is that in the United States of America, many of these people see their dentist regularly. In 2013, 47.2 percent of adults 30 years of age and older had mild, moderate, or advanced bone loss (aka periodontal disease), as did 70.1 percent of adults 65 and older.[1] That study has not been updated, but the general anecdotal evidence suggests this number is increasing, not decreasing.

As periodontal disease rises, so does the difficulty in working with insurance companies for those with the luxury of coverage (I use the term *coverage* loosely as their contribution often leaves people feeling naked, not covered). On the professional side, 85.6 percent of dental hygiene services completed are D1110s (prophylaxis). Disease recognition and case presentation are not currently reflective of disease prevalence. Furthering the discord, 7.5 percent of the registered dental hygienist (RDH) workforce left clinical care from the years 2020 to 2022. Burnout among RDHs is at an all-time high. Fast-as-you-can "scaling and root planings" are masquerading as bloody prophies.

In summation, we have a good and proper mess on our hands. Before you chalk me up to be a Debbie Downer, I should note my deep commitment to optimism. I believe that the darkest moments produce unprecedented strength and beauty. Therefore, what I love about the messy situation is that there has never been a better time to make a positive change. A change with tangible, worldwide potential for profound and lasting impact is at our fingertips. It will take contributions, big and small, from us all. I believe it starts in our own hearts and operatories. If we can normalize true prevention, early disease recognition, and individualized care, we could clean up a huge part of this mess.

Once we clean up our own operatories, we can move to the community, state, country, and world at large. We must prove to ourselves that an effective way to help our patients achieve health *is* possible. That will translate to passion and energy for service on a grander scale, and the number of 3.5 billion people with oral disease will suddenly begin to drop. Hallelujah! Healthier, happier smiles and immune systems are a dental professional's dream come true!

We will learn how to uncover exactly what each individual needs and move from herding cattle to providing exquisite, individualized care. We will ditch the age-old patient education that hasn't worked in forever. We will build a case for a total body health approach for dental care. Get excited to gain the tools needed to execute all of this effectively. Once we have mastered individualized care in our own operatories, get ready to watch the spread of goodness.

I am delighted you are here with me. Together, we will have the best time cleaning up dentistry's act! The joy of a healthier you, patient, and practice will be a brilliant blessing without end. Herding dental patients like cattle will be a distant memory. Get ready to enjoy your career more than you ever thought possible.

What do you want to be when you grow up?

It's the million-dollar question we all get asked from primary school on. How on God's green earth can a kid know how to answer that? What I should have said was "fulfilled." Instead, I got nervous and sweaty. This type A, firstborn, people-pleasing overachiever had to rise to the challenge of that incredibly misguided, inappropriate question. I searched far and wide and had life figured out by second grade. I was going to be a model. I didn't tell a soul this was my plan. It was a good thing because, in the fourth grade, I was riding my bike with no feet and crashed into the double-pane window in the front of my house. My purple sparkle helmet saved my life, and the seventeen stitches in my chin ruined my dreams of a career as a model. My tear-stained, nine-year-old self had to find a new life plan.

Back at the drawing board, I asked thousands of questions of anyone who would let me. I spent many hours talking to my Uncle Steve, who happened to be a dentist. It was in those chats with Uncle Steve that I found my calling. At the ripe old age of thirteen, I made the big decision. I was going to be a dental hygienist. I thought, "They make tons of money, have a totally flexible schedule, and don't have to go to school for very long. Brilliant." I had a plan. Little did I know that my assessment was highly inaccurate. I was about to embark upon a journey for which the money was good but not the tons I expected, the schedule was locked in six-plus months in advance, and my education still has not ended.

Down the path, I went. I became passionate about taking care of people. The dream of health and happiness sat center stage in my heart. I acquired a bachelor's degree and an RDH license. I began to practice with everything I had. As a graduate of Idaho State University, I believed I was ready and well-equipped to be one of the best clinicians ever. I quickly gained skill and speed and tried to be extra fun, so the patients would love me. I felt it was a privilege to care for each human entering my operatory. As the first and only dental hygienist at a brand-new office, I had the freedom to develop my own hygiene program. I am delighted to report that both healthy patients and super diseased patients received incredible care from yours truly!

As the years went on, I began to realize that a huge portion of my patient population was becoming more diseased, not less. How could this be? I removed all the calculus, checked my work, and asked Dr. Eron for help when needed. (He is left-handed, which means excellent access in hard-to-reach areas for us right-handed clinicians. This is a dream tag-team tartar-removal situation). I encouraged good brushing and flossing until I was blue in the face, over and over again. Then I realized the problem. To quote Taylor Swift, "It's me, hi, I'm the problem, it's me."[2] Sure, I used my best patient education abilities to teach good skills and encourage quality habits. Still, I threatened my patients, telling them periodontal therapy would be the consequence of not complying with my recommendations. I neglected to teach them how to read X-rays. I only spot-probed (and not necessarily at every appointment). My commentary to them often included things like, "You have a little bit of bleeding today…" and "We'll get you all cleaned up and it'll be just fine…." In my effort to save people time and money and to avoid talking about a topic I thought would hurt their feelings, I swept disease under the rug.

Did you catch how that whole last paragraph was all about me? What I did. What I wanted. My fear of being honest with my patients. I was the antihero. Clinical care was all about me and my best efforts. Nowhere to be found was patient autonomy. Missing was patient accountability. Absent was collaboration.

While I did not know the specifics of what was missing, I knew something was. I began searching for a remedy. Then, one day, I was sitting in class at the Utah Dental Association Convention, and a light bulb went on in my head. My beloved patients were getting diseased under my watch, and their inflammation was a systemic issue that was causing havoc for their entire body. I was not only allowing disease to grow, but I was also encouraging it. In class, I felt truth in my soul when the speaker said, "There is no such thing as a little bit of bleeding. Either there is bleeding, or there is not."

Upon further digging, I was re-enlightened to the fact that 30 to 50 percent of bone density is gone before we can see it on X-rays—making any radiographic evidence of alveolar destruction a BFD (big freaking deal). Next, as long as the care was about *me*, it would never be successful. People needed to be autonomous and decide for themselves whether they had disease. They had to choose if they cared to do anything about it! Wow. Talk about a shock to the system. There is nothing quite like the feeling of trying to do something helpful only to realize the "help" has been a complete hindrance. (Are there any parents in the room? Surely, I have a friend or two in the crowd. 😊)

My next career phase was dedicated to continuing education (CE) and a new way of practicing dental hygiene. I developed an assessment routine that gave my patients the tools to diagnose their disease. My team and I worked hard to use verbiage our patients could easily understand. We also unified our efforts so that everyone was on the same page clinically and received the support required to implement the new approach.

In a very short amount of time, everything changed. My days became more manageable. Instead of "Brandi sweating through her lab coat doing bloody prophies all day long," I had time and energy to provide exquisite care. I also was able to take lunch breaks. I stopped talking until I was blue in the face about home care. I quit taking responsibility for the health or lack thereof of my patients. I freed myself and them from a system that simply did not work.

You might be wondering, "What happened?" Well, the same people that I feared wouldn't like me anymore if I gave them bad news thanked me for the best care they had ever received. They invested time and money into their dental needs. They started taking responsibility for the care they needed. My schedule reflected the time required to care well for each person. The people who were already in our practice were grateful for updated information. New patients raved about the quality of care they received. Rather than disease increasing, it shrank. Instead of sweaty nerves, my team and I enjoyed the feeling of excitement for progress. The trust of my patients soared. The hygiene department became exponentially more profitable. Everybody won.

The new version of practice filled my soul so full that I realized this, like a light, was not meant to be hidden under a bushel. It was meant to be shared! So, here I am, sharing this light (aka recipe for individualized patient care). This will improve the health and wellness of the patients, providers, and practices that utilize the recipe.

To be clear, this recipe is not the *only* one that will bake up a healthy result, but I share it because I have found unprecedented success with this recipe as a clinician, team leader, and coach. The tools you will find in this book are repeatable and effective. They are meant to be used in service to yourself, your patients, and your practice. Half-hearted, half-a$*ed approaches will likely fall flat and add to your frustration. Read on if great days, healthier patients, and a profitable practice sound like everything you've dreamed of as a professional. I'm so glad you're here. If a little humor and clinical excellence sounds lame, it's cool just to pass. I will not hold it against you and will cheer for your success and fulfillment either way.

If you're sticking with me, let's get to it!

Brandi Hooker Evans
April 2024

Chapter 1

It's All Greek To Me

Do you know that glazed-over look teenagers get when you share the list of expectations for their behavior? Particularly when you are leaving town, and they get to stay home alone overnight? The one where their face is directed at you, and their eyes are open, but their ears are off? Behind their eyes, running like a ticker tape is: "Yeah, yeah, feed the dog, lock the doors, no parties, I got it. When are they leaving? Does the credit card bill show if we get soda? As soon as they pull away, this day is going to rock!" It is as if we were speaking Greek to a non-Greek-speaking human.

That is exactly how our patients feel when we discuss their health on our terms. Here is what I mean: dentists, think back to dental school. Did you shakily label tooth anatomy for that first test and cringe when you had to choose an appropriate material for each procedure? Dental hygienists, get your memory out too. Did you cross your fingers while naming all the instruments for the first time? Did all of the acronyms make you cross-eyed and sweaty? Truly, the vocabulary necessary to make it through school equated to a full foreign language! Where the heck are our extra credits for such toil?

Instead of the teenage ticker tape for stay-home-alone evenings, our patients' version sounds like this: "Yeah, yeah, yeah, I need to brush and floss more, my gums are bleeding, get the power toothbrush, try the water flosser, lean in so she thinks I'm listening, add a head nod or two just for good measure…."

By using our terminology, we are immediately removing ourselves from our patients' team. We have placed ourselves in a position of power, thus losing a measure of trust. Consequently, open communication cannot exist. We then rely on our acting ability to get people to "accept treatment." I say pass.

We can eliminate the language barrier in the dental office by dropping the teeth geek lingo. I love that you know modified glass ionomers are ideal for protective restorations. I'm so proud of you for knowing that mesial starts with m, like midline, and is the side of the tooth closest to the center of the mouth! And I know you have the vocabulary to explain periodontal disease at a microscopic level, but you guys, trust me when I say, "We don't sound smarter. We lose our audience."

Instead of trying to *impress* patients with our dental prowess, check out the steps we can use to *empower* our patients to diagnose their own gum disease:

1. Keep all explanations simple enough for a fourth-grader to understand. This step is a rule that will rock your life in preventive *and* restorative dentistry. I love fourth graders because they are big enough to "get it" without talking

down to or patronizing them, and a fourth grader will not have the vocabulary of a dental or dental hygiene school graduate. Albert Einstein is said to have proclaimed, "If you can't explain it simply, you don't understand it well enough." I am inviting each one of us here to understand it well enough to put it simply!

2. Never, ever, ever—I mean *never*—skip any part of the big five of assessment: medical history and update, blood pressure reading, oral cancer screening, radiographs, and full mouth periodontal chart, including bleeding points at all six locations of every tooth. No matter how tempted I am to skip it or how far behind I am, I have learned that this is the portion of the appointment where each patient's needs become crystal clear. If this isn't your jam and you decide to skip anything in this section, have fun with your bloody prophy. Call me when you are burnt out, and we can chat again. How do I know you will call? Well, because *yours truly* started out as the struggling RDH needing a plan that worked!

3. Show each piece of the assessment to your patient. Hey! Y'all! This is their mouth! While we are tempted to bust out the ready-made patient education material, they do not care about a beautiful picture a textbook company made or a fabulous flip chart a toothpaste company made. No, they've got skin in the game. (Ha! Pun intended.) So, explain what's in it for them. They must look at and learn from their own X-rays, blood pressure readings, perio charts, etc.

Here are some helpful one-liners for you to try out and use as you see fit. Plagiarize or modify; certainly, I have had plenty of help honing these in over the years. I started with explanations like "the oral-systemic link has been associated with significant hindrances to our immune systems, an increased risk for periodontitis as well as heart disease…" Friends, they were lost at oral-systemic. *So*, try these on for size:

- **Medical history and update:** "Your mouth is connected to your body. I can help you take great care of both if we know what we are working with."

- **Blood pressure reading:** "Heart disease and gum disease are often related. They can help or hinder one another."

- **Oral cancer screening:** "We are going to start with an oral cancer screening. Let me know if anything is sensitive." (No further description is necessary. If they ask for more information, give it to them. For example: "I am feeling for lumps and bumps. I want to know what is normal for you and if there is anything that we need to investigate further. I have helped a lot of people identify thyroid issues early. No matter what we find, the earlier we discover it, the better outcomes are.)

- **Radiographs:** "This thick white line of bone should go up, over, and down between each tooth."

- **Periodontal charting:** "One to three millimeters is normal, and healthy gums don't bleed or hurt while I measure."

Say that out loud with me, "One to three millimeters is normal, and healthy gums don't bleed." Ten extra points if you say it out loud again. Excellent!

When the assessment is complete, we sit the patient up and review the information together. We will not, I repeat, will not tell them they have gum disease. We will deliver the objective findings in terms a fourth grader can understand and then pause. That's right. Shhhhh. Be quiet. What is next? Can I get a drum roll, please? Nine times out of ten, our patient will ask, "What are we gonna do?"

Ta-da! Yay! Yes!! What are we going to do? This is your moment to jump in with fabulous news!!! "We know just what to do! We are a team and are going to treat this disease. It will require you (the patient) and I (the dental professional) to work together with a new plan moving forward for home care as well as professional care." Friends, fill in the blank after that. All that worry about case acceptance: gone. What is not to love about this plan?!

Now that we've stopped mixing dental "Greek" with English, we can really start to thrive.

Welcome to the end of the chapter! Here is where you get to reflect and evaluate. For Chapter 1, jot down the patient you had most recently who seemed to be pretending to listen while you shared about their health and dental solutions. Then, consider how the conversation might have gone to have more impact. Was it fewer words? Was it less complicated? Or perhaps it needed a different direction altogether. By the way, I still have this conversation with myself even after having practiced in this "not herding cows" way for quite a while. #WorkInProgress

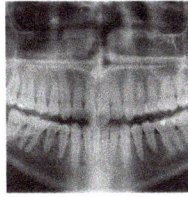

Chapter 2

Donkeys And Dentistry

*N*ever skip the assessment because to assume is to …. (Look up the rest of that saying on the internet. I'm gonna keep it classy here. 😉)

Drop the assumption that your patient is "healthy," and get curious. The Big Five steps of assessment are just that, *big*. They lead to nonnegotiable, must-have pieces of information required to take excellent care of these humans we love. We touched on them, and now it's time to dive deep. Ready?

Medical History

Earth-shattering information right here: our bodies are connected to our mouths. And our mouths are connected to our bodies! Speaking in plain terms, this relationship is a two-way highway where information zooms back and forth all day, every day. The knowledge gathered during the medical history review aids our ability to guide the patient in a direction that is pertinent to them. For example, Jill marked "yes" next to Sjögren's syndrome. We should perk up like dogs on the hunt after a twig snaps. Our next thoughts might be:

1. Autoimmune disease, dry mouth, dry eyes, extreme tiredness, careful with the cotton, higher risk for caries and periodontitis, slower healing time, higher levels of stress hormones, and difficulty achieving homeostasis.

2. I wonder what Jill is specifically struggling with.

3. How can I tailor the products and practices to Jill's specific needs today?

My favorite trick is to recommend milk with meals. Milk of any kind, not just cow's, has the ability to lubricate the mouth, making chewing and swallowing comfortable and enjoyable. It also provides nutrients needed for the cells to be successful in every body process. Remember, Jill has an immune system that is attacking healthy cells and making it hard for her to live well.

Recently, I had a patient, we shall call him Jerry, who came in for his "seven-month perio maintenance." You know, he had had to cancel his three-month appointment and had thought, It's no big deal. I'll just wait until the next one.

Jerry is taking Lisinopril and Zoloft. I asked about side effects, and he stated excessive thirst, then proceeded to share about his health journey. As of April 29th, 2006, Jerry claimed to have lost and found 240 pounds. Currently, he is 50 pounds down from his original starting weight. I celebrated with him and kept gathering data.

At the end of perio charting, he said, "That's the worst one I've ever had." Because he was doing rather well with his home care (for example, floss picks in his truck, at his office, next to his bed, and in the bathroom), he had cause to be shocked by his perio chart.

Here was my response: "Jerry, I have an answer for you. Do you want to hear it?" After an affirmative reply, I said, "What this will take is *you* going all in on *you*. We know that it takes three months for the bacteria that cause permanent destruction to repopulate after a professional dental hygiene service. The infection in your mouth is being dragged through your entire body, making everything from your immune system to your hormones and, consequently, your mood suffers. Likewise, your body is at a disadvantage in healing your mouth because it is taxed in multiple ways. This means that the places you cannot reach at home have had seven months to build their house and party on."

Jerry exclaimed, "They (the pathogenic bacteria) are @$%-holes, and today is their eviction notice!"

Yeehaw! The bottom line of this unexaggerated replay (because I could use Jerry's medical history, total body health journey, and the information he already knew to help him commit to himself completely) is that I armed him with knowledge about the oral-systemic connection. Jerry was shocked to hear this but said it all made perfect sense. He commented that our conversation was exactly what he needed for motivation to modify. By the end of the appointment, he left *sans* the subgingival calculus and biofilm (thanks to my trusty ultrasonic), *plus* the belief that he is capable of taking care of his health. I did not reprimand, I did not say the same things over and over, nor did I coerce him.

I believe nearly everyone is capable of positively caring for their own health. As such, it is my (our) job to empower them, deliver usable information, encourage an effective plan, and be the support group. Jerry is not a unique experience. As he left, he said he wished more people cared like I did. I think they do. I just think we have not had the tools to do it differently. The "prophy mill" with "cleaning ladies" running it is several decades old, and as I write this in 2023, it is the only book I know of its kind. Granted, you can find articles, coaches, and CE classes with similar roadmaps to success. However, these principles are not widespread knowledge and practice. Thank you for reading and being a part of the #ChangeWeWishToSee.

Appropriate Radiographs

Fifty points for the first person to text me what ALARA stands for. And one thousand points for the one who can illustrate why the radiation required for digital dental films has become a nonissue. Gone are the days of "not for pregnant women" and even lead aprons. Feel free to check your local laws before you join the 2024 dental standard of radiology. When you're ready, ditch the apron because digital radiographs have reduced scatter radiation to nil. At nine inches past the exposure point, the radiation completely dissipates. It is time to come out of the dark ages of dental radiology. Hey, ISU grads before 2009! Remember Tab can demos with Anita? Remember when we used to think life would be so easy once we graduated?! Ha! We were wrong. Oh, so wrong.

All right, back on track.

What we need is a great view between each posterior tooth. Thank you transillumination for those anteriors. We also need a picture of every tooth's roots. (Hmmmm. Is it teeth roots or tooth's roots? I don't know what the correct plural-ness of that is!) Split hairs about a seven series, a full mouth series, a panoramic film, or a cone beam computed tomography (CBCT) scan all you like, but I am going to roll forward with my personal favorites:

- Pano: A panoramic film provides an amazing overview and a great oral cancer screening and alerts us if further films are indicated. Take a new one at least every five years.

- Four bitewing X-rays (BWX): Please take four great horizontal or vertical bitewings with open contacts and a clear picture of at least three millimeters of the interproximal bone. We need to see the cortical bone and go down into the cancellous bone to make a quality diagnosis. If you take a bad film, cuss, then retake. By the way, know your audience! Don't say $#!^ out loud if you deem it inappropriate. You can always cuss inside your own head. Remember: Austin Powers had no inner monologue, but you can! I digress again, back to it.

- Three Anterior PAX: Anterior periapicals are fabulous. Take two of the upper anterior (capture canine to central on each side) and one of all the lower anteriors. We can catch all kinds of disease on these films. Where do people generally build calculus that shows up on the X-rays? Lower anteriors and molars! Also, where do people lose bone first? Lower anteriors and molars! Bada bing, bada boom! We have the information we need to diagnose and present well to the patient.

If you want more information at the end of your appointment's X-ray exposure section, get it! Snap a retake, add a periapical, or go back and grab that CBCT scan. Radiation exposure: minimal.

Information gathered: priceless. Please use your best judgment. Your favorite X-rays can be different from mine, but the intent and information are the same.

On to the best part of the whole dang chapter! I love to use this magical phrase when I show my patients their stunning radiographs: "Do you see this thick white line? It should go up, over, and down between each tooth." Translation into dental Greek: the dense cortical bone should follow the one-millimeter radiolucent line of the periodontal ligament, fully encapsulating the softer trabecular cancellous bone. The average amount of density lost before it is visible on the film is 30 to 50 percent. That number is decreasing with every advancement in technology. The critical idea is that we see cortical bone density. If there is density reduction, we have to B-E Aggressive! Or, go ahead and watch disease develop, telling ourselves that six months and another prophy will do the trick.

I also use the phrase, "Do you see where that line is gray and fuzzy? We see a bleeding five-millimeter pocket when we match it to the gum chart. This is telling us that the infection is beginning to cause permanent damage. What is great about catching this right now is that we can restore the bone's strength! There is no height loss yet, which is excellent because we can't regain height."

Another helpful trick is to find a place in the patient's mouth where the bone looks healthy on the X-rays so they can see the difference. It gives our patient a reference point in their own mouth. I recommend using their own X-rays every single time because the flip charts and other patient education tools that are not the patient's own mouth are largely useless. I realize that is a harsh generalization and judgment. However, after many years of practicing myself and implementing this with other clinicians, it is safe to say that you can burn each and every one of them. You do not need them. Just throw them away. Less clutter, less mess, more blessed!

Blood Pressure Reading

You might be thinking, "Ummmm pass. I don't even want to take a blood pressure. It is dumb!" Well, I have had a total of four middle-school-age children, making me competent in the verbiage behind that "look." It's the same look I get when I teach a class or coach a dental team and state, "Taking blood pressure is *non-negotiable.*"

Y'all, I get it. It is one more thing, but is it? Heart disease and gum disease are besties. We lose 800,000 Americans to cardiovascular disease every year. Do you know what they find in the clogged arteries? Freaking *P. gingivalis* and *Aggregatibacter actinomycetemcomitans.* What on Earth! You bet your @$% those are the gram-negative, stinky, inflammation-causing perio bacteria. The heart pumped blood to the infected gingival tissue, which was contaminated by the little sh!^$, and then they cycled back through the body, causing myriad responses. This includes putting an extreme tax on the liver, causing it to release inflammatory cells such as cytokines and low-density lipoproteins, which what? Oh yeah, clog arteries! My friends, we must connect the dots on this knowledge in our minds and hearts. This is the only way we can make the difference we are being called to make.

In 2014, I completed my own anecdotal study while creating my company, Stellar Outcomes. For six months, I tracked "out of the normal range blood pressure" and "dental hygiene services needed." In that time, every single patient who needed more than a "six-month prophy" had hypertensive blood pressure readings. Many of them had never had their blood pressure evaluated, let alone acquired a diagnosis. That is a lot of firsthand experience, adding to my evidence-based decision to take a blood pressure reading at every single appointment.

Added bonus: I am like that lawyer building an ironclad case for the patient's need for advanced dental hygiene care. By the time we complete the assessment, scaling and root planing with perio maintenance appointments every three months for life is the only rational choice the jury or, in this case, the patient could ever make. Even better is when they decide three-month prophies are the best course of action to prevent the dang destruction from occurring in the first place.

Another added bonus: this is an opportunity to reinforce our role as someone who cares and is qualified as a health care professional rather than "just" a dental nurse. By the way, I use all of these incorrect names lovingly. Nurses and janitors (aka cleaning ladies) are amazing, and I wear both titles regularly. I simply aim to state that we are not *just* anything; frankly, neither are the janitors nor nurses. No matter our position, we have the choice to operate at our full potential or be *just*. This applies to every position in every profession. Let this be the spark in our world for all of us to own our incredible ability to make a positive and lasting impact anywhere. Any time. Period. 🧡

Oral Cancer Screening

In 2013, two of my dental pals were diagnosed with thyroid cancer. Had the cancer gone unnoticed, it would have taken their lives.

Today, they are both healthy and well, thanks to early detection. One of them, Liz, is the first dental assistant I ever worked with. She dealt with all things thyroid cancer, then went on to dental hygiene school—woot woot! Now, she is back at Evans Dental. We share patients and send each other funny memes as our primary form of communication. We dream about meeting up for a run, a glass of wine, or both, in no particular order. I am beyond grateful to have her in my life. Imagine how her husband and two wonderful children feel about the professional who found her cancer. I hope never to be the one to find oral cancer. More importantly, I hope never to be the professional who missed it.

Here is an example of how easily we can incorporate this into our routine:

"Hank, we are going to start with an oral cancer screening. Let me know if anything is sensitive or bothers you." It is best to keep this explanation simple. It is common for hygienists to overexplain what they are doing if it is something new or something making us uncomfortable. However, Hank does not care about our rationale behind this part of the appointment. If he does care, he will ask. In that case, it is absolutely reasonable to say, "I want to make sure that everything looks and feels normal for you. If trouble of any kind arises, catching it early is our best chance for success."

During the oral cancer screening, take note of Hank's coloring and symmetry; check his lymph nodes and jaw. If Hank's jaw ever hurts, this is an excellent time to brainstorm about what is causing the pain and how to remedy it. Often, a simple ten-to-twenty-minute walk at the end of every day is helpful enough to relax Hank into a more peaceful state of mind and a more restful night's sleep. Obviously, that is not the only way to help people with temporomandibular disorders, but many people just need to chill the freak out so their TMJ will feel better.

In our culture, we tend to overlook highly effective medicines such as taking time to let the amygdala rest, enjoying nature, and moving our bodies. Suggesting a walk after work to help Hank's jaw pain shows him we know a thing or two about whole health and that we care. Have you ever heard the adage, often attributed to Theodore Roosevelt, "People don't care about how much you know until they know how much you care?" That is exactly why we are taking our time to do a thorough assessment.

We also want to know what Hank's thyroid is like. Out of the estimated 20 million Americans with thyroid disease, 60 percent of those people are unaware they have trouble. For many people, we are the only health care professionals to palpate the neck. It is typical for men to go decades without a health physical. Depending upon the type of health care provider a woman has, her primary care physician might not check her thyroid either. This is further evidence that we (dental professionals) must make a thorough effort for these patients we love.

Once we have observed and palpated Hank's face, jaw, and neck, it is time to lean him back and look inside. Does he have petechiae on his soft palate? What do the insides of his cheeks look and feel like? Does he have white, lacy, lattice lines on his cheeks? If so, perhaps Hank has lichen planus that we need to help him address.

Is there anything noteworthy in his vestibule or under his tongue? Speaking of his tongue, how does it look and feel? Is there anything abnormal with the shape, color, or texture? Does it appear that his tongue is resting in a place that indicates trouble breathing, eating, or speaking? We are learning that the tongue tells more of the story than we originally thought. Wink, wink, pun intended.

Are Hank's saliva glands working? How big are his tonsils? Does Hank struggle with strep throat, allergies, or sleep apnea? Maybe myofunctional therapy is the best next step in Hank's life.

During this visual and tactile exam, we have the opportunity to catch trouble. The earlier, the better. #EarlyDetectionSavesLives

Moving on to Hank's hard tissue. Are his teeth worn down to little nubbins? Does it appear that he has scrubbed his teeth so hard that much of the supporting structure is absent? Or how about methamphetamine use? Does Hank have black, bombed-out teeth that suggest an addiction to drugs or Mountain Dew? Are the insides of his teeth eroding, indicating GERD or an eating disorder? And when Hank bites down on his back teeth, does his occlusion look healthy? Personally, I have had many adult patients seek orthodontic care because their occlusion was causing trauma to the hard tissue and devastation to the soft tissue. We can treat perio pockets all day long, but if we never get to the root cause of the issue, such as traumatic occlusion, we will never succeed.

Full Mouth Periodontal Chart

The moment we have all been waiting for: *the perio chart!*

"Hey Hank, one to three millimeters is normal, and healthy gums don't bleed or hurt while I am measuring." P.S. Pus is bad. 😉 Once the probe depths and bleeding points have been recorded (at all six locations of every tooth), we need to know about recession and furcations. Does Hank have clinical attachment loss causing mobility? Let's write that down, too. While we gather this information, we must say it all out loud. If we do this, we never have to tell Hank he has periodontitis. He will tell us by the end of the assessment (the whole point of this book).

After we call out the perio chart, we are going to sit Hank up and show him the radiographs. "This thick white line should go up, over, and down between each tooth." The thick white line is his lamina dura. But Hank doesn't need a new vocab word right now—he needs to know if his thick white line is intact or if the spots that were bleeding are also losing bone support. If so, Hank is going to ask us for perio therapy in just a second because *bleeding and bone loss are the signs of active periodontal disease.* He will tell us that he needs treatment as a prevention activity is no longer appropriate for him. He would like a healthy mouth and body and better breath.

Super cool note: that "thick, white line" trick also applies to enamel. "Do you see that fuzzy, dark, V-shaped notch? That is where a cavity is starting." Who knew reading X-rays was such a cinch?!

At this point in the appointment, Hank is likely super impressed. If we've done our job, he feels loved and cared for. Maybe he is excited to go on a walk right after work and thrilled we can help him heal his periodontitis (which he diagnosed all by himself). In addition to being grateful for incredible care that he has never experienced before, we have high hopes that Hank will be loyal to us and his health. We may not have made it to the tartar picking today, but Hank needs four quadrants of scaling and root planing. A bloody prophy would have harmed him more than helped today. Ergo, we saved the day and his future. Congratulations, RDH! What an honor to be on the same team.

Quality assessment is the key to fulfilling clinical hygiene days. Now more than ever, our patients need us to get to the root cause of their ailments. They need to believe that we care deeply for them and are here to serve. The brilliant part of quality assessment is that this whole routine takes less than twenty minutes to complete. All five steps of medical history, blood pressure reading, oral cancer screening, radiographs, and full mouth periodontal chart are a breeze. That leaves twenty-five minutes for calculus removal, polishing, and double-checking our work and fifteen minutes for the exam. If what Hank needs is a prophylaxis, this system does not make us run late. If Hank needs something else, we now have the data to support the necessity of more time and more involved dental hygiene care. The result will be a healthier patient (Hank), a healthier provider (you or me), and a healthier, more profitable practice (our respective clinic).

Yeehaw!!! Let's do it.

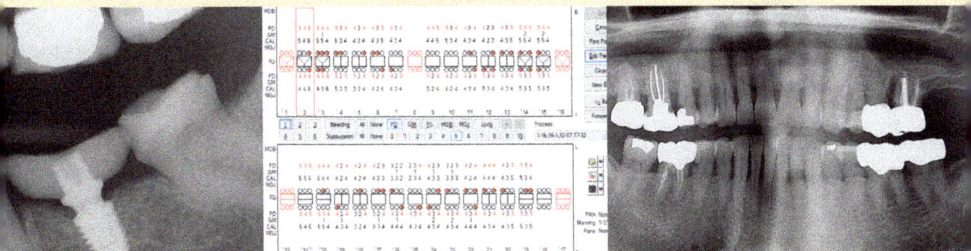

Ogres are like onions, and donkeys love parfait. Just like Shrek, our patients have many layers to them. But does it matter? On this reflection page, please consider the other side of my argument. Is there anything you can actually skip? What if the patient is late? Scribble the devil's advocate side to what I have just shared with you. Is the case for knowing our patients' layers holding up after we are missing assessment items?

Chapter 3

Case Presentation
(More Like Case Shushing)

*W*elcome to this chapter! Here, you'll find the golden gem of my entire journey as a dental professional: the secret to case presentation.

Dental peeps have searched far and wide for this—from CE classes to books to the Dead Sea Scrolls—hoping one of them would have the answer. The treasure we sought was the critical piece to dentistry that, when done right, would ensure the patient's health and the practice's livelihood. This is what I call pure unicorn dental magic.

What can we say to convince the patient that the treatment plan we so carefully crafted is what they need, want, and will do, starting today?

Drumroll, please. The answer is nothing.

Shhh, be quiet, *silencio*, no talking. Just give them a freaking minute, guys! Our darling patient just gained a new skill in periodontal disease diagnosis and realized that they have it!

That's a lot to digest. If the silence feels awkward, try to enjoy it. If you can't, ask a basic, open-ended question such as, "What do you think about the data we've just collected, Bob?" Spoiler alert: Bob's going to say, "Dang it! This is bad news. I have gum disease." Right, you are, Bob. Right, you are.

As educated, experienced dental geeks (oops, dental gurus), our job is to give the patients the tools they need to decide for themselves that they have disease and want to do something about it.

If we tell our patients they have gum disease, they have much more mental work to do. They have to question if they believe us. They have to decide whether or not they care. They have to decide if their understanding is adequate. However, if they tell it to themselves, we have buy-in that cannot be reproduced in any other way. This is spectacular self-discovery because now they are more likely to improve their home care habits and attend their re-care appointments.

At this point, case acceptance is 100 percent. The patient presented and accepted their own case. Now, we have the privilege of offering the options that will serve them the very best.

People have time, money, and motivation for what they value. Period. If that philosophy does not fit within your belief system, then let's challenge what I've said.

According to the American Pet Products Association, Americans spent $136.8 billion on their pets in 2022, an increase of 10.68 percent from 2021 ($123.6 billion).[4] Per *Forbes* magazine, "Dog owners spend an average of $730 a year on their dogs."[5]

Let's play devil's advocate. Our sweet patient Juanita has no resources of any kind. No credit, no service or product to trade, nothing, nada, zilch. I say, take a move from the Nike playbook and "Just Do It!" We all took an oath and swore to give back to the community and those less fortunate than us. We can be dental missionaries on the rare (trust me, it is rare) occasion that someone does not have the ability to garner the resources to pay for dental care. I know countless professionals who pack their bags to leave the country and serve people without resources all over the world. Not only do the people in those countries not pay for the care, but the dental professionals pay their own way! My friends, just because someone lives near us doesn't mean we can't do a mercy mission for them in our very own comfortable office.

All right, I know, everyone has an eyebrow raised and is unsure if this is a good plan. I get it. You think that, according to my philosophy, you will be paying to do dentistry all day, every day. On the contrary, with this case presentation style leading to almost perfect case acceptance, you will find that free care is rarely necessary. I recommend doing this for one person per month in a "one doctor, two-to-three dental hygienist" practice. We shall name them our "patient of the month." If you want to see your career satisfaction go through the roof, let your patients diagnose their own disease and then serve one human a month with scaling and root planing or a few fillings On The House. Who knows, you might love it and get wild with a full-mouth reconstruction case that will change the patient's life and yours. Forever.

Man, I am good at going on a tangent! To sum it up:

1. Show your patient you care.

2. Do a complete quality assessment.

3. State the facts of disease during each step of the assessment.

4. Display their data.

5. Shush...be quiet.

6. Stay quiet.

7. When they ask, "What are we gonna do?" line out treatment plan options and let them choose.

8. Celebrate.

9. Get to work.

10. Repeat with the next patient. ❤️

Do you believe that your patients can diagnose their own periodontal disease if you remain quiet? What would it be like to try this on for size for thirty days without fail?

Chapter 4

When They Ask You

*Y*ou did an excellent job collecting the assessment. Your explanations were simple yet spot on. You survived the awkward silence. You sherpa'ed Bob to the golden pinnacle of patient autonomy. He has diagnosed his own gum disease and wants to know, "What are we going to do?"

Congratulations! Wahoo! This is it! The moment you never knew you were dreaming of! Bob paid attention during your assessment process and diagnosed his own gum disease! These moments are priceless and never get old. Now that Bob says he has gum disease, we have to decide what that means in regard to billing and coding appropriately based on the extent of his disease.

Before we move forward, take a deep breath. Soak in the gratitude possibility for Bob to live a better, healthier, potentially longer life—if not at least a better-smelling breath. One more deep breath while you consider the following items (in your own head):

1. Look at each quadrant separately.

2. Count the teeth that have bleeding and bone loss (this is our parameter for disease beyond gingivitis).

3. Bill the quadrant appropriately. One to three teeth have bleeding and bone loss; use code D4342. Four or more teeth per quadrant: D4341. Take care of two quads today and two quads next week.

4. Keep in mind that removing biofilm, plaque, calculus, and stain from the entire quadrant is included in the 4341 and 4342 codes. There is no need or ethically sound reason to bill a prophylaxis. So, if you find yourself feeling tempted to bill a prophy along with any scaling and root planing code, take a little advice from Elsa and "Let It Go!"

Reminder: the above is an inner monologue. Think Austin Powers. Below is an example of the out-loud conversation we could use to explain to Bob how we proceed:

"Well, Bob, it's real simple from here. We will treat the areas that need treatment and prevent disease in the areas that need prevention. See this chart and these X-rays? We will count the number of teeth with bleeding and bone loss in each quarter of your mouth. Those numbers tell us what codes to use for insurance purposes. We will take care of half today and the other half next week."

You can add in things like, "I'm so excited you're here today. This disease will never be easier or more affordable to treat than it is today." Or, "Your whole body is gonna thank us for kicking this infection!" Or, "We're going to make a great team. I'll do my best here; you do yours at home, and together, we'll rock it!"

In reference to "doing their best at home," I highly recommend suggesting just one thing for them to work on. Preferably something that will address inflammation and its effect on their whole body. We want to drive home the point that this isn't merely a local-to-the-mouth issue that we happen to be on a "kick" about. This is, in fact, an infection that is negatively affecting Bob's entire body!

A word to the wise on treating patients with insurance: do not bill more than two quadrants per day. Period. Chart every piece of information you gather and ensure your notes are brilliant (see an example of my auto note and letter to the insurance company in Chapter 11.2. Include findings from the perio chart, risk factors, active infection, and any medical history items. This will allow your notes to paint a comprehensive picture of what is happening in Bob's body. It also shows that Bob is a real human with concerns that warrant care.

If I were in a lecture hall right now, seventeen of you would have your hands up and want to stop *here*. The insurance can of worms hath been opened, and there is a need to discuss it further. If your hand is up, I'm going to highly encourage you to pause Chapter 4 and read Chapter 11 on Freaking Finances. I'll be here with bells on when you get back.

Okay, here we are. Because every patient is not a "Bob," let me give a few more examples:

Perhaps Suzie has localized early periodontitis in her upper molars. The conversation may sound something like this, "Great news, Suzie! We have caught this disease in its earliest stage. We will treat these two teeth on your upper right and these two on your upper left. Let's do everything we can to boost your immune system. In three months, we will make sure that there is significant healing happening. You said that work has been wild lately. One way to help your mouth heal and lower the effects of a busy season at work is to walk at the end of the day. Where is your favorite place to stroll?"

Or, maybe Zack, the college kid, has acute necrotizing ulcerative gingivitis. "Zack, your immune system is totally pissed. Let's get a great plan to calm it down and get you feeling good. The more rest you can squeeze in, the better. I know that it is super hard doing school. What do you think would be a good plan to get more sleep?"

What if Marietta has had prophies in your office for the last twenty-four years? "Marietta, you have done such a great job coming in regularly to care for yourself. Because we have signs that our previous plan is no longer meeting your needs, let's make a new plan. To support your ongoing commitment to wellness, we should start treating the infected areas today. Let's pick one area of health to focus on. What comes to mind?" Marietta looks at you strangely. You go on with, "I know it sounds different than the usual brushing-and-flossing speech, but we are finding more success when we give the whole body what it needs to heal. Certainly, feel free to grab that water flosser you've had your eye on, but let's look at the bigger picture and do an even better job caring for you."

It's reappointment time after you've worked your instrumentation magic and had the best home care conversation possible. Periodontal Maintenance D4910 is always every three months. *Do not waffle on this!* (If you can't wait one more minute for pro tips on reappointing, put a bookmark here and flip to Chapter 9). 😉

If you went to Chapter 9, welcome back! If you have to read the book in chronological order—I see you type Aers out there. I totally would not have flipped to Chapter 9 yet, either.

Let's put a bow on this concept. When Bob, Suzie, Zack, and Marietta ask what we need to do for their periodontal disease, give them your best recommendation for care, both here at the office and at home. Look at all of them as if they were precious treasures of your heart. Give the same recommendations you would for your own family members. Sincerity will come through in spades. I used to be worried that they would leave upset. I have learned that they will shake your hand or hug you and say, "Thank you for taking such good care of me. I have never experienced this at any other dental office." Talk about career satisfaction! I get teared up just thinking about these moments. I hope you enjoy each and every one of them.

Think about the last five clinical days you worked. Is there anyone who could have used a different treatment plan? If so, what would it have been? If not, which patient was the trickiest for you? What did their treatment plan entail?

Chapter 5

Whoa, Whoa, Whoa!

*M*aybe you're thinking: *My patient absolutely did not ask me, "What are we going to do?" Brandi, you are carrying on like you're perfect, and this plan solves everything, every time, period. And you said assuming makes you an a$$, so if the shoe fits, maybe you should slip it on, Cinderella.*

If so, then whoa, whoa, whoa, time for a step back. I want to share another side of me—hoping these concepts will become more real to you.

I love yoga. For years, I had a mellow mat routine. I was not practicing with any real dedication or attempt at improvement. The new gym I was going to offered yoga on Tuesday nights. I showed up to the first night expecting a feel-good flow; I proceeded to get my booty kicked. As an overachiever, I love to follow directions and do exactly what the instructor calls out. Or more. Well, the yoga instructor, Waylon, made that impossible. Halfway through the warm-up, I was looking around for salt to season the humble pie I was apparently going to have to eat. During Savasana, I laughed (almost silently) while I lay like a sweaty lump on my mat, wondering, "*What the heck just happened to me?*"

It did not take long for Tuesday nights to become my favorite night of the week. I always had that pre-hard-run-jittery-tingle in my belly. Call me a masochist, but I craved it. I made friends that I now deem besties. My family moves mountains to ensure I am available for Tuesday night yoga. My children and husband even join me on occasion.

Every week, I show up and honor my body. I have learned to love right where it is. I have found there is no end to a yoga journey. There is always a next level to achieve. And though I may not be able to do eka pada bakasana (one-legged crane) "correctly" this week, I may next. Or it may be next year. Either way, I'm going to love my body and my practice. I will laugh when I crumple to the floor in the thousandth attempt to execute a pose.

Waylon didn't ask me to leave class when I couldn't keep up. He kept giving me instructions for proper alignment and encouragement to achieve the next level.

When my patients show up to their hygiene appointment, I meet them where they're at. I hope that they will be ready to attempt the next level of health. However, if they aren't, it's a big fat freaking "high five" for showing up today. I am going to love them where they are. I am going to allow them to decline the treatment they need today. I am going to hope they want to come back and spend time with me again. And, because I am loving them well, they are going to trust me with their care time and time again. When they reach the tipping point, when they finally decide they are not willing to live with this disease, I will be there. No "I told you so" or reprimand. Simply there with a smile and my favorite ultrasonic tip.

This book is a story and an account of my dental hygiene experience. Some people are not ready to move forward today, which is okay. I did not even attempt many of the poses Waylon called out that fateful first Tuesday night so many years ago. What I did was keep showing up. It took months to decide that I would *try* the more advanced poses, let alone set a goal to achieve eka pada bakasana or adho mukha vrksasana (handstand). Happily, I can do both now. Our patients are no different. They can get healthier if they want to and if they stay dedicated. Sometimes, it just takes more than one invitation to try a handstand or a power toothbrush. 😉

I realize there are a hundred other ways to approach this situation. Many dental professionals become aggressive and offended. They demand signatures on the declination of treatment forms and attempt to shame a person into submission. While I love a good declination form and encourage its use for those who would like to, I do not believe in shaming our patients. Ever! If you choose to use a declination form, ensure you do so with dignity and kindness.

To be clear, I believe every single patient has the right to quality assessment and treatment plan options. Options for operative and hygiene care should always include "do nothing." I also believe if a patient asks me for a service that will "do no harm," I will happily provide it for them. In the event that Johnny needs periodontal therapy but asks for a prophylaxis, I clearly state that the service is inadequate for the disease present and that it will not prevent the disease from progressing. However, I am delighted to do what Johnny has asked.

This is where I use whatever time I have left in the appointment to ultrasonic the mouth, and I finish at the scheduled time. I run prompt for my next patient. What I do not do is sweat through my lab coat, do four quads of scaling and root planing, lie on the bill, and run late the rest of the day.

When Johnny leaves, I wish him well and silently pray that next time he will decide to upgrade his life and health. As Johnny walks out the door, he takes responsibility for his own health with him. I do not carry that weight on my shoulders. I did my best, and that is good enough. Hopefully, next time, Johnny will try that new pose. ❤️ I also hope that my delivery improves to ensure our friend Johnny acknowledges his disease and is ready to practice in a more healthful way.

Practical advice: do not judge your patients. Educate them. Love them. End on time. Schedule them back in as few months as they will agree to so you can educate and love them again! #LongGame #PartnersInHealth #Rapport #LoveThemAnyway #Namaste

To my dearest yogi pals Hailey, Tina, Meg, and Waylon,

I had no idea that attending 7:00 p.m. yoga would be a profound life decision. Really, I thought I was showing up for a trivial workout that would leave my body and brain as soon

as I exited the "Barre Pocatello" studio. It turns out you were all about to become one of the most precious treasures of my heart.

Hailey, for the longest time I didn't know your name. We talked, laughed, and crashed on mats right next to each other for weeks with your name in my head as "Friend." Your strength, courage, and athleticism are gorgeous. Thank you for always supporting me and our classmates. Also, you're the most incredible mother, and I love Thad like he's my own nephew. Give him a high five, a squeeze, and an attaboy for me. 😉

Tina, speaking of amazing mamas, it's no wonder Hailey is so good at it. She learned from you! Your bright light and love are an example to me (and everyone around you). My soul is filled full while in your presence. I feel seen, heard, and wanted simply by your pre-class hug. I also love that you keep me posted on the cow cuties at your farm. The way you care for animals is another testament to how great of a soul you are.

Meg, I was feeling so lonely for girlfriends when I first came to your classes at the Barre. All my friends were busy like me or lived far away, making regular base-touching sporadic at best. The business you created and your genuine openness and ability to connect played a crucial role in my life. Thank you for being a bad@$$ entrepreneur. I take the gifts your business provided and your friendship in my heart everywhere I go. You've made such a positive difference in the world.

Waylon: the guide of all guides. Somehow, you always seem to know what we need physically and mentally. We all feel so lucky to have world-class, professional, profound, healing, challenging, fun, and empowering yoga experiences right here in Pocatello, Idaho. Thank you for serving our community so brilliantly. The impact you have made and your friendship are more meaningful than words can articulate.

The four of you are absolutely wonderful. I can hardly write these few short paragraphs because my heart is bursting with gratitude, and I can't see through the tears that are welling up and escaping my eyes.

Lastly, to all the yogis I've had and will have the honor of practicing with on this earth, thank you for sharing such a sacred experience with me. I hope you take a ray of light from me to brighten your days and add hope to your world.

Namaste.

Sincerely, your yogi sister,

Brandi

What do you love to do? Is there something you used to do and don't anymore? What could you add more of to bring health and wellness to your weeks as a fabulous dental professional? I challenge you to make a date with yourself and keep it—no matter what. 😋

Chapter 6

Doing It For
The Mooooo-lah?

That will be one meeeeelllionn dollars (insert Doctor Evil's diabolical laugh and pinky finger up to the corner of his mouth). Where are my Austin Powers fans? All joking aside, what does a quadrant of periodontal therapy cost in your office? Really, what does it cost? Is the health benefit your patient will gain worth that? Are the skills and expertise you have worth that?

In comparison to other goods and services, is your price reasonable? My hope is the answer is a resounding "Yes. The care I provide is worth ten times what we charge."

Let us be clear that this system of caring for the patient will fall flat on its face if done with money as the motivation. The work we do and the system we use must come from a place of abundance and service. The yuck factor will come through to Alex if you are trying to make a quick buck. Depending on his personality, Alex may complete treatment today, but he will not be back. Alex also will not be sharing you with his friends and family. Loyal patients are far more valuable to the practice than a constant stream of "one-off" new patients. Do not forget that if Alex does not return, we will not see him heal and achieve his health goals.

Another reason to get comfy with recognizing and treating periodontal disease early is periodontal disease will never be more affordable or easier to treat than it is today. In other words, today, my services are cheap and easy. Tomorrow, they will get pricey! Isn't it amazing I can wiggle a "Hooker" joke into just about any scenario? 😉

If treatment takes less time, costs less money, is more comfortable, and is more effective, why wouldn't we treat it today? Suffice it to say that if Alex presents with bleeding and bone loss, it is time to treat the disease. That is not greedy. That is honest. The entire purpose of a prophylaxis is to prevent disease. If you are providing periodontal therapy but calling it a prophylaxis, that is a lie. It is also considered fraudulent. The direct comparison is the dentist performing a root canal while telling Alex he's doing a filling. That is never alright, nor is it okay for the RDH to perform nonsurgical periodontal therapy while telling the patient it's a prophylaxis.

Plus, Alex wants to know what's up.

The go-to rule of thumb for diagnosing is to ask yourself these questions: "Is there bleeding and bone loss? If so, where?" Count the teeth in each quadrant that have *both* bleeding and bone loss and code correctly. Boom! Problem solved. Not using greed, just sound judgment. Let the healing begin! In conjunction with Alex's healing, your practice will be healthier, too. #EveryoneIsWinning

A side benefit of quality care is profitability. Even small hygiene departments can be exceptionally profitable when quality care is the center of the system. Bottom line: the reason to take exquisite care of your patients is not the money. It never will be. Fortunately, the money just shows up as a reflection of the disease butt-kicking you and your team are doing. #AwesomeJob!

Is the care you provide worth the amount of money and the time that it takes to complete it?

Chapter 7

KISS

$\mathcal{A}$re Sixpence None The Richer singing to you, too? "♫Kiss me out of the bearded barley. Nightly, beside the green, green grass. Swing, swing, swing the spinning step. You wear those shoes, and I will wear that dress. Oh, kiss me.♫"[6]

This is officially your inspo to KISS often! It looks like this in the dental office: Keep It Simple, Stupid/Silly/Sunshine. At my house, we crack up and use "Stupid," but that feels a bit crass, so let's go with Sunshine. Keep It Simple, Sunshine. I like to be called Sunshine, so thanks for working that aloud with me. 😘

There is a wide spectrum of periodontal condition presentation. Unfortunately, there is not a matching set of codes to bill our patients. I am always jealous that those of you who are dentists have a variety of codes to bill for fillings based on the extent of the decay. What I wouldn't give for a one-, two-, three-, or four-surface filling code that reflected the extent of disease.

Alas, we must do the best with what we have. My request as we proceed is that you take a fat, black Sharpie and write "bleeding and bone loss" somewhere you can see it every day. Active disease is best discerned by bleeding and bone loss. If we use that mantra, diagnosis- and care-planning become cinches.

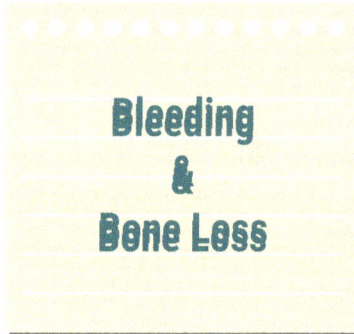

Bleeding & Bone Loss

Here are a couple of examples of patients we see every day. They come in a wide range of health and diseases:

Adeline: No bleeding on probing (BOP). One to three millimeters probing depth (PD). Model-perfect bone on radiographs. Bill: D1110–prophylaxis!

Bruno: Localized BOP lower anteriors. One to three millimeters PD. Excellent radiographic bone health. Bill: D1110! It's still **a prophylaxis!**

Claire: Generalized BOP. Two to four millimeters PD. No radiographic evidence of permanent damage. Bill: D4346–scaling with gingivitis, and D0180–comprehensive periodontal exam.

Darren: Localized BOP. Two to four millimeters PD. Radiographic evidence on upper molars of permanent damage with widened periodontal ligaments (PDLs) and crestal bone density reduced. Bill: D4342 teeth #2–3, D4342 teeth #14–15, and D0180–comprehensive periodontal exam. Nothing else!

Now that Darren has entered periodontal therapy, we do *not* bill prophylaxis codes anymore. Darren is now in periodontal therapy and will need to follow the appropriate protocol until we have radiographic confirmation that his periodontium has healed completely. This requires at least one year of three-month periodontal maintenance procedures and a new set of films to ensure that the bone is completely healed. If, at that point, there is zero bleeding upon probing and scaling, the PDLs are normal, and there is restored health in the interproximal bone, then you can consider going back to a prophylaxis.

I have been a dental hygienist with my very own license since 2007. I have had almost no one meet those qualifications. I realize it is a tall order and I'm also trying to communicate that *we must be more proactive if we truly want to prevent disease.* If we do not want to see refractory cases, then we have to stick with the plan that works. One of my favorite lines is: "What we're doing isn't working. We need to find a new game plan." Well, the fact of the matter is, now we are doing what's working, so why would we mess with that? This idea of saving time and money is only appropriate if health isn't our overarching goal.

Edna: Generalized BOP. Three to five millimeters PD. Radiographic evidence of generalized widened PDLs and crestal bone density reduction. Bill: D4341 in all four quadrants (two today and two next week) and D0180–comprehensive periodontal exam.

Frederick: Generalized BOP. Four to seven millimeters PD. Radiographic evidence of generalized interproximal bone height reduction. Bill: D4341 in all four quadrants (two today and two next week) and D0180–comprehensive periodontal exam.

Gwen: Sporadic BOP (50 percent). Four to eight millimeters PD. Marked radiographic evidence of permanent bone loss. Current smoker. Bill: D4341 in all four quadrants (two today and two next week) with a special note in the chart about smoking risk factor as well as the danger of vasoconstriction masking the true disease state and D0180–comprehensive periodontal exam. (At the three-month periodontal maintenance procedure appointment, we will do a reevaluation with the potential for a referral to the periodontist as further treatment will likely be necessary).

Let's make it really simple. Follow the checklist below, and you will accurately diagnose disease every time.

Keep It Simple Sunshine

* Assess the assessment *

1. Is there **bleeding upon probing**?

    a. If no—high fives all around. "Great job!" Move onto discussing your patient's hobbies.

    b. If yes—red flag. Move to the next step in diagnosis.

2. Is there **bone loss visible on the radiographs**?

  a. If no—since bleeding is present, infection is present and must be addressed. You might say, "This is great news! We can completely restore health for you!" Then consider giving one recommendation your patient can make between visits to support their immune system—and skip the brushing/flossing lecture. If gingivitis is in the severe category, switch to a three-month prophylaxis routine for prevention.

  b. If yes—count the teeth and provide nonsurgical periodontal therapy (NSPT) for the teeth affected with both **bleeding** and **bone loss**. (Use codes D4341 and D4342 as needed.) Make sure to remove plaque and calculus from *all* the teeth. Perio code verbiage includes the NSPT *and* the prophy. In other words, bill the appropriate number of teeth for NSPT and care well for the whole mouth.

And *voilà!* A simple, two-step answer for a stupendous assessment!

Does Keeping It Simple Sunshine sound like a breath of fresh air to you, too? Good luck! This "bleeding and bone loss" sticky note has changed my life, and I hope it blesses yours.

Chapter 8

Clean Up That Stinkin' Mess!

*Y*eehaw! We've figured out exactly what type of care Karen (our newest patient) needs. We finally get to blast calculus and demolish the biofilm!

The hygiene treatment routine that rocks my world, allows me to chat too much, and finish early, follows.

Where is the worst calculus? The entire crowd sings: "The lower anterior linguals!" Right you are, team. 😉 And that shall be where we begin. Choose the correct ultrasonic tip for the type and volume of deposit present. Test your choice by tapping that tartar, baby! If the calc comes off easily, you know you have the correct combination. Ultrasonic those lower anterior teeth until you believe they are completely free of deposit. Move on to the surfaces toward, and finish with surfaces away. Rinse and repeat for the maxillary teeth. Then, switch ultrasonic tips for a slim or thin attachment and proceed to use it like an explorer. If and when you find deposit that the first tip missed, simply activate this thinner tip. Stay with the calculus until it is completely removed. Floss the teeth as an additional round of exploration. Polish and apply fluoride. Voilà! Hygiene routine elevated and simplified!!! Use at least two ultrasonic tips per patient. As more complicated conditions present themselves, use the appropriate and as many tips as you need to complete the task well.

Do not hesitate to grab your doctor or another hygienist in your office for a second opinion on hard-to-reach or tenacious areas. Post-op films are a brilliant idea as well. Removing the deposit and biofilm is only one step of the healing process, however, it must be done well. I used to believe that experts don't need help. Now, I realize experts are always open to a second set of eyes and hands. ❤️

Should you require the use of hand instruments, start with a sharp instrument and go waaaayyyy back to the basics. I can still hear Denise "Nina" Bowen, my darling mentor from dental hygiene school, telling me, "Bite, release, in the tooth, then up the tooth, that's it, bite, release, one-millimeter strokes." While on the root surfaces, remember that pressure will gouge the root, making the job impossible to finish. Feather-light crosshatching strokes are the ticket to success when we are down deep in the pocket abyss.

I adore my posterior Graceys and miss them from time to time. Not enough to go against the evidence about cementum removal but, alas, I am getting ahead of myself. Hang tight on that idea and keep reading until the end of this chapter. For now, just know I love those posterior Graceys, and if, for any reason, ultrasonic instrumentation is contraindicated, I bust them out with glee!

At school, I learned that most refractory cases could be traced back to one simple skipped step: exploration. Nina imparted sage wisdom about double- and triple-checking our work. Try exploring with an ODU 11/12, a very thin ultrasonic tip (names range across brands), floss, and post-op films. Most of where we work is inaccessible to our eyeballs, making these adjunct tools a must.

If I find deposit while exploring, I let my patient in on the information. I show them a clean spot and then go to the spot I missed. I ask them if they can tell the difference. Most quickly get on board with me and affirm when I have achieved complete removal. Hint: they just got a floss lesson and a reason to be diligent at home. I may have only spoken to them about "finding veggies," but my actions gave them a unique experience to consider along with their home care regimen. #HighlyRecommend #SneakyRDH

Cleaning Up That Stinkin' Mess Simplified:

1. Assess the type and volume of the calculus.

2. Choose the appropriate ultrasonic tips. It's tempting just to use one, but we can do better, so get two tips out before you begin.

   a. Start with the "big guns." These vary by brand and whether you are using magnetostrictive or piezoelectric technology (if you use a Cavitron ultrasonic, this might be your blue tip).

3. Add a finer tip to finish and explore with (maybe green or purple).

4. Start in the lower anterior lingual area. If deposit does not easily and efficiently come off, stop. Adjust settings or get a different tip for the calculus.

5. Remove calculus from all surfaces you can reach at each clinician position (eight o'clock, nine, noon, etc.).

6. Switch to your thin, exploration-capable ultrasonic insert. Explore everywhere! Tap that foot pedal to activate when necessary.

7. Floss to check again.

8. Check the clock and be shocked at how speedy and effective you just were.

9. Celebrate!!!!

I also like to finish with polish and fluoride. We could argue about whether or not to do those two things until the cows come home. Here's how I see it: polish is my favorite part of a hygiene visit. For every study that says we should not polish, there is one that says we should. Fluoride is also controversial in some circles. Based on my research and experience, I like it and recommend it. The benefits are well-documented and profound. It is also very cost-efficient. The key is to ensure our patients aren't eating the fluoride as a snack. It is bad for you to swallow a bunch. 😉 So, until we have data on something better, varnish is my go-to for many of my patients. Just like my instrumentation style, it is subject to modification should the necessity arise.

"Do the best you can with what you know. When you know better, do better." Thanks, Ms. Maya Angelou. #WeAreWorkingOnIt

Speaking of knowing better and doing better, instrumentation is an area of dental hygiene care in which I have made sweeping changes. I have been exposed to irrefutable evidence that the way I learned to instrument, the "blended approach," is inferior to what I'm about to share with you.

If I asked how many of you use the blended approach, the majority of the room would quickly and proudly raise their hands. I would then ask, "How many use hand instruments only?" A few sheepish hands would come up. And, finally, if I asked, "What about ultrasonic only?" There would be crickets until I popped up my hand to say, "After years of working on it, in April of 2023, I finally achieved my goal of *ultrasonic instrumentation only* for the majority of my patients!"

The crowd would be aghast—because, forever and ever, the preferred method of ultrasonic-ing around for a few minutes and then finishing up with a sharp hand instrument has been the epitome of excellent clinical instrumentation. But here's the rub: that style of care is more time-consuming, more damaging, and less effective than ultrasonic only.

Ultrasonic Instrumentation Is Less Time-Consuming

The blended approach is more time-consuming because we do not utilize the ultrasonic to its full capability. We are then scaling and root planing everywhere with hand instruments. By the time we are using an explorer and the floss to check our work, a tremendous amount of time has passed.

Here is another big fat freaking reason to reconsider our beloved hand instruments: they need to be sharpened every ten to twenty-five strokes for typical calculus and every three strokes for heavy tenacious deposit. Meanwhile, many of us wait until our instruments cannot cut through room-temperature butter before we elect to sharpen them. And then we cuss at them throughout the entire appointment, repackage them, autoclave them, and then find them again tomorrow! Commence with more cussing. Really, it's a feedback loop of negativity we could just skip nearly 100 percent of the time.

Ultrasonic Instrumentation Is Less Damaging

Here's why: hand instrumentation takes off ten times more cementum than ultrasonic instrumentation. Check out the comparison in this picture! Thanks, Dentsply Sirona, for finding and sharing such incredible motivation for change! Look at how close the curette removal is to the diamond bur removal! Yikes! We are removing calculus for periodontal healing, not prepping the tooth for a filling.

Cementum Removal By Instrument

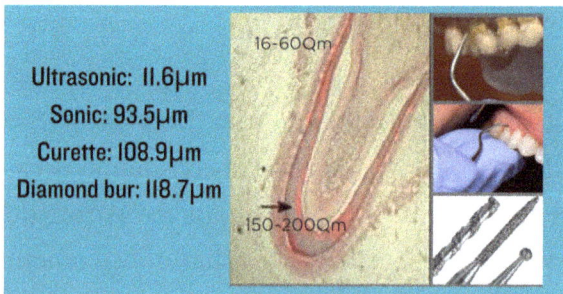

Ultrasonic: 11.6μm
Sonic: 93.5μm
Curette: 108.9μm
Diamond bur: 118.7μm

16-60Qm

150~200Qm

When our best recommendation for many patients is to come in every three months, removing cementum by hand instrumentation is wayyyyyyy more damaging than we would hope for. This is especially pertinent for our patients with recession.

Ultrasonic Instrumentation Is More Effective

The dental world is buzzing with the latest information around comparing biofilm removal of ultrasonic versus hand instrumentation. Research at the University of Glasgow found that ultrasonic instrumentation disrupted and removed 50 percent more biofilm than hand instrumentation. *Fifty percent!* Ladies and gentlemen, that is a tremendous reason to modify our subgingival dental hygiene instrumentation approach. Not only does the ultrasonic remove 50 percent more biofilm, but it removes one-tenth of the cementum.[7]

That, my friends, is a double whammy (see 1980s *Press Your Luck* game show for good, clean fun and comprehension of that reference). Yeehaw for ultrasonic instrumentation!

We also must look at the effectiveness of our care. Much to my chagrin, check out the research:

> "Waerhaug evaluated the effectiveness of subgingival instrumentation on a sample of 'condemned' teeth and concluded that the chances of removing all subgingival deposits are high in pockets smaller than 3 millimeters. In pockets of 3-5 mm, the chances of failure are greater than success, and in pockets larger than 5 mm, the chance of failure to remove all deposit dominates."[8]

OMG, guys! How many of us are waiting to even chat about perio until after five millimeters? Ugh! Why not treat the disease rather than the pocket? The first time I read that article, I nearly barfed. I have worked really hard to be an excellent clinician. I pride myself on thorough and gentle care that removes all deposit.

Sadly, I cannot see in the subgingival workspace without a fancy camera. Even though the research shows that our effectiveness decreases in deeper pockets, we can mitigate that issue. We must do our best at the initial treatment appointment by utilizing the ultrasonic to its full potential and follow up at twelve-week perio maintenance (PM) intervals. Those PM appointments are our chance to check our work and ensure Michael gets the healing we anticipate, given his risk factors and compliance.

In school, Nina always taught us that most refractory cases can be avoided with the simple use of an explorer. Not to mention, twelve weeks is the average amount of time virulent microbes need to repopulate—now *that* is some major motivation to implement care to our patients at the earliest signs of disease *annnnd* follow through with long-term success plans.

Dear Nina,

Thank you for guiding me through dental hygiene school. Thank you for not missing a single one of my milestones as a licensed professional before you left this world. I thought we were just getting started. Turns out, you were prepping me and so many others to take the baton and keep striving for better.

Remember my first week of dental hygiene school? Mari, Steph, and I crashed your first date with Tommy. Ha! Hazards of sharing your plans with college kids. We were always available for procrastinating homework. 😊

I love that you taught me how to scale and root plane as we sat with my sweet Auntie in junior clinic. I truly feel like I learned from the best of the best and with someone so dear to my heart. Priceless. You probably didn't hang onto this memory, but I failed my first care plan in your class. Eeeeeek! You taught me failure was simply an opportunity to become stronger. You made me think about what kind of clinician I wanted to be and lit a fire under me to work hard to achieve any goal I have.

The level of accountability and excellence you held me to throughout the program were foundational and appreciated. A few years later, you held my hand as I became president of our state hygiene association. We often laughed over mimosas at brunch, and you cheered me on when I started my business. You inspired me to strive for excellence, and bought the champagne after my master's defense. By the way, thanks for being my graduate faculty representative. 😉 You were instrumental in the success of that project.

I miss you. I hope you know there are so many of us carrying on your legacy. Your love resides in our hearts. Your contribution to our profession and our lives continues to be profound.

I love you so much,

Brandi

Try it out! Use this page to write about the first three times you go for "ultrasonic only" instrumentation. Was it fun? Was it faster? Did you feel great about using the latest research to upgrade your clinical care?

Chapter 9

"Whatever it Takes"

♪♪ ♪ ♪♪ ♪♪I hope Imagine Dragons is playing in the back of your mind as you read this chapter.

Like seriously, whatever it takes. I was coaching a team that had a patient named Ramone who was battling lichen planus. Three-month recares weren't cutting the mustard. I mean the calculus. 😉 We looked at all the information for Ramone and decided that an efficient ultrasonic instrumentation every two months was a great place to start. We wanted to minimize cementum removal and maximize biofilm control while keeping Ramone comfortable during his hygiene visits. We also recommended Magic Mouthwash for flare-ups (half Benadryl, half Maalox, shaken and refrigerated, swish and spit three to four times per day as needed for comfort). Is this a regular recommendation? No! Is Ramone a regular patient? No! Ramone's oral health greatly improved, and the dental appointments became more comfortable. Ramone is also now that practice's number-one fan. He recommends them to everyone he talks to.

We must consider each case individually. The game plan for a relatively healthy thirty-year-old with few to no additional risk factors and excellent plaque control will be completely different than one for an immune-compromised, raging bleeder with multiple risk factors who builds calculus bridges in three months.

Let's break it down.

Remember when we used the line, "What we are doing isn't working. We need a new game plan?" This is our chance to find one that does work and then back it up. For example, we complete scaling and root planing and begin three-month recares. After twelve months, we have eradicated all the bleeding. This is the time to stick with the plan. This is not the time to stretch out the recares. It's way cheaper and easier to high-five and full-mouth ultrasonic than it is to backslide. I suggest using "Wahoo! What we are doing *is* working now! It's great that we found the right plan for you!"

Refractory cases suck and are made worse by them being our fault (at least partially). It takes twelve weeks for the virulent bacteria to repopulate and elicit an immune response that causes permanent destruction. Therefore, our job is to help our patients see the value of quarterly attendance to the chair of their favorite RDH (that's you and me, pal). Please, oh please, do not try to save your patient money at the expense of their health and inflammation.

Once we go backward, it is hard to regain trust. I try to be ultra-transparent during the whole process from start to finish. I'm always positive and hopeful, but as sheer as nude pantyhose, about what the body is doing.

If we are in an uphill battle, I set goals like "reduce bleeding by half." Taking Suzette from 168 sites with BOP to eighty-four is a win! I'm alright with eighty-four BOPs because we are in this for the long haul with Suzette. Not to mention, reducing 168 sites of bleeding upon probing to zero points of bleeding upon probing in three months is something I have never witnessed in my seventeen-plus years of clinical practice. It's unrealistic to expect immediate and perfect healing in three months.

Many of these people have been working on developing periodontitis for many years, decades even. Getting the habits, immune system, and bacteria back in check takes time. I liken the process to getting in shape. Ten push-ups don't give you buff arms, but ten push-ups that grow to twenty, thirty, and forty every day absolutely produce very strong arms over time. Add variables such as diet, other physical activity, body type, quality sleep, and joy levels, and a person can really make a monumental improvement in their fitness. It takes many small steps over time to "get in shape" or "eradicate periodontal disease."

What I'm suggesting: choose not to be alright with results we can improve upon. Mediocrity is one root of burnout. If we are giving options, our patients can choose for themselves. Why not have the ideal option in the mix? We also need to remember that our goal is to get ahead of Suzette's disease and improve her overall health. Being proactive rather than reactive motivates her to follow through on other areas of her life. What we are working on is deeply multifactorial. The more motivation to follow through, the better. Controlling for the brushing and flossing factor is great, but self-care, nutrition, sleep, deep connection, and movement are also profoundly impactful. This is our chance to shoot for the moon so that if we miss our mark, we still land in the stars. Suzette agrees.

Alert: The most common mistake I see my hygienist friends make goes like this:

1. Scaling and root planing (celebrate!)

2. Periodontal maintenance (yahoo!)

3. Signs of improvement (heck yes!)

4. Stretch out recares (what? nooooo!!!)

5. Battle a refractory case ($h!^, $h!^, $h!^)

It is a vicious cycle. It happens repeatedly. Let's skip that drama and stick with evidence-based recare intervals. Twelve weeks is the sweet spot. Think of it as a dental hygiene dessert. Finish off with raspberry polish and caramel fluoride varnish as needed. 😉

The alternative:

1. Scaling and root planing (celebrate!)

2. Periodontal maintenance (yahoo!)

3. Signs of improvement (heck yes!)

4. Three-month recares (nice!)

5. Continued improvement (woot woot!)

6. Lifelong success and support (that's what it's all about 💖)

Have you heard of Rella Christensen's research on the one-month polish program? She brilliantly observed the profound effects on patients of simply polishing one time per month. The reduction in inflammation was incredible. Patients with special needs, those who are failing cognitively and physically, and struggling teenagers are all great candidates for this practice. For those who need special help, their caregivers are incredibly grateful for extra support. In nursing homes and treatment facilities, brushing is a battle that is often lost (or not even fought). Our goal is to disrupt the biofilm so that the virulent bacteria can't colonize and mobilize. For non-compliant teenagers, one-month dental visits are a fantastic wake-up call to "get your act together." We have had many parents require their "plaquey" teenagers to foot the bill for the additional dental trip. Now *that*, my friends, is an express highway to better cooperation! #HighlyRecommend

We do this one-month polish program (which we call "modified recare interval") for dozens of patients in our Idaho practice. It's a sixty-minute appointment where the hygienist uses the ultrasonic and polishes—no hand scaling. Nobody has insurance that covers it, but each patient who opts in is happy to pay out of pocket.

One of our current peeps is a sweet little blue-haired lady, Edith, who comes in for her monthly ultrasonic and polish. Her daughter brings her and is grateful to tears every time. Edith is struggling with Alzheimer's disease at eighty-eight years old. It takes all the workers at the memory care facility, plus her daughter, to keep Edith going each day. Unfortunately, toothbrushing has been bumped to the bottom of the priority list. We are keeping her gingival disease in check with monthly hygiene appointments. I thank the heavens above every time I get to take care of her and walk her out to the car. I always pray that someone will do this for my granny if she ever needs it. And quite frankly, for me, if I ever need it.

For every patient who sits in our chair, let's ask ourselves: "What would be ideal?" Craft a good, better, and best list of options and let them choose which suits their values. Keep in mind that "doing nothing" is always an option, too. My experience has been that the patients will take the professional's lead. If *we* are wishy-washy about treatment and recare intervals, *they* will be wishy-washy about treatment and recare intervals, too. And if *we* won't take a refractory case for an answer, well—you get the idea.

Who in your practice needs one-month recares? If you are caring for elderly and ill folks, know that I am sending you peace and gratitude. Who else in your practice could use more frequent appointments?

Chapter 10

Team, Team, T T T T T T Team, Team, Team

I n Italy, it is customary when ending a phone conversation to say, "Ciao, ciao, ciao, cha cha cha cha cha cha ciao, ciao, ciao," all the way from the end of the chat to the slow motion of pushing the telephone's end button. The Italians simply cannot say it enough! That, my friends, is exactly how I feel about teamwork and hygiene departments. Team, team, team, team t t t t t team, team, team.

First and foremost, if there is a kink in the team hose, the flow will be blocked. Simple yet true. Yeah, yeah, yeah, B, I heard that before. I know you have heard it, but have you lived it?

Let us examine the team a little more in depth.

At both ends of the patient experience is the administrative team. From website chats and answering phone calls to entering our building, this section of the team creates the first impression for every patient. They give the humans *we hope to care for* the vibe of the practice. Every administrative team member needs to be able to answer the phone and discuss the nature of periodontal therapy with simplicity. Imagine this:

"Hi, Christine. I see that you are working with Dr. Evans and Kelli to treat gum disease. The cost and time for those services are different from the preventive cleanings you've had in the past. I'm so glad that you are choosing to take care of yourself by doing this. Nutritious food, sleep, and exercise will help your mouth heal more quickly. So, feel free to be all about self-care to get the most out of your care here!"

The administrative team is also in charge of our schedules. Dental hygienists, let's not hygiene diva our way into an irritated and unsympathetic administrative team. There is simply no reason to ostracize them. The secret to supporting the administrative team is to be kind. "Please" and "Thank you" go a long way. Spend time sharing your expertise and learn about them as humans and professionals. Taking a few short minutes to be appreciative and connect with them will make all the difference. Rather than trivial, think monumental. Try it. I have yet to see these tips be a waste of time. Barring a bad apple, kindness wins every time.

Moving right along to our pal, the dentist. "But my dentist doesn't blah, blah, blah." Guess what? It is likely that your doctor feels the exact same way about their hygienists. I am going to cut straight to the point. The time has come to draw a line in the sand and step over it. The old war of doctors against hygienists and vice versa has got to stop. Leave all that baggage in the past. Let's go, team! You are *the* team, not simply "a" team but *the A-Team*.

Want to know how to step across that line? Check it out:

1. Have a professional conversation about the people you both care for so deeply (your patients).

2. Ask what they would like to see for hygiene care.

3. Share your hopes for catching disease early and preventing it with vigor. Examples include three-month prophies, whole body health, varnish application, etc. (More on this later!)

4. Read X-rays and perio charts *together* like it's your job—because it is! Y'all, we are the diagnosis team. The more we compare notes, the more they match. Matching is fun. Trust me. 😉

In my years as an educator and dental coach, I have learned that most people want the same thing. Our titles and different licenses do not change that. Pitfall per the hygienist: "I did all that, and my doctor isn't interested." I hear you! First up, you need to get really curious and find out why. Likely, there is a barrier to success that can easily be removed. For example, the dentist feels that patients will not care or that they will be upset. In that event, offer to try this new approach (wholeheartedly) for ninety days and then reconvene. At that point, if the program is not going well, the two of you can renegotiate how to proceed. Spoiler alert: your hygiene department will be on fire in ninety days! That troubleshooting sesh you offered will never happen. As a bonus, your dentist will feel refreshed and revived. Their career will improve. They will be elated to see their patients begin caring for their health. Notice I did not say "oral health" because the healing will be so much more. We are talking the whole enchilada *mi gente* (my people)! Just think of hundreds of healthy enchiladas running around your town, feeling fabulous and smiling with much less plaque on those teeth!

I saved the best for this moment: the assistants. I know, I know, I love everyone equally, just in different ways (says the impartial mother duck about her ducklings), but assistants are the best.

In all reality, who do the patients go to when they aren't sure what the doctor and hygienist said? The assistants. Who do our peeps ask whether or not they should get the treatment? The assistants. Who cleans your room when you are running behind? The assistants. Who charts when you need a hand? Who converses during wait time in the operative chair? Etcetera, etcetera, etcetera, y'all get my point. The assistants are the connective tissue of our teams. They are also the trust keepers. Not sure if this is true? Observe a team with a powerhouse assistant and another with a ho-hum assistant. I am confident you will then be able to write the rest of this chapter on the significance of your assistant team.

Having an efficient and well-educated assistant will afford you the opportunity to perform your job well and support your efforts in empowering your patients. For many of our patients, this is the first time they've heard anything about brushing and flossing in any style besides "Charlie Brown's finger-wagging teacher." Also, it is likely the first time they realize how much power they have over their own health trajectory. I have found that a killer assistant is the key to a killer hygiene department. Equip our assistants with basic periodontology information and a "thank you" or two, then you can step back and watch them ensure the success of our whole practice.

Continuing down our team line, let's address the other RDHs on our team. If you want to sabotage all your hard work with me here, please throw them all under the proverbial bus. Talk crap to your patients and the rest of the team about them. Also, be sure to note in the chart the date and film showing where they missed a piece of calculus the size of Texas. Make sure your patients know that the reason they have gum disease today is because Stacy missed it. *Awwww, dude*—that ain't the way to do it. *Mind you*, we have all missed calculus and a diagnosis. What we do is *practice*. We are all doing the best we can with what we have at the time. The trick is sticking with Ms. Maya's sage wisdom: when we know better, we do better.

To modify this dynamic, begin with a safe conversation, as previously stated in our example with the dentist. Continue with quality continuing education. Follow up with team lunches that include case studies as often as possible. It will not take long to sync up and feel like the unstoppable team you were meant to be. Remove the threat, blame, and assumptions, and there will be no ceiling to stop y'all in this magnificent patient care endeavor!

Lastly, my darling new friend, *you* must get on the team. No matter your title, dentist or hygienist, the team needs you. If you are not on the team, this whole program will fail. Like all relationships that work, everyone must contribute. This is our chance to shine as a service guy or gal. Hygienists: learn how to answer the phone. Better yet, know how to cover Aubri up front when she has to work through lunch. Get comfy with that danged high-speed suction so Betty, the assistant, can grab a snack.

Doctors never underestimate how powerful it can be to do dishes in the sterilization room and help with operatory turnovers. Jumping in to do a task that isn't "yours" is a super-secret special sauce that everyone should know and practice.

And double lastly (is that even a thing? Ha! Now it is), be on your own personal team in your mind. Be confident! This is life-changing information for our patients. They need us to *own* our expertise like the health care professionals that we are. Nobody wants surgery from a surgeon that is *kinda* going to make an incision, then *maybe* do a little work, and *hopefully* sew them back up. Heck no! The dialogue should sound like: "We are going to help you. The procedure will include x, y, and z. It will take x amount of time. We can expect healing given the following conditions…"

One more thing, will you *please* solemnly swear to stop apologizing for the amazing care you know how to provide? No more, "I'm sorry to deliver bad news." It's, "I am thrilled we have a great plan to take care of you! It will never be easier, less expensive, or more effective than it is today!"

Once everyone on the team works well, we can achieve incredible success in every category. Part of caring well for your team is to heed the following advice: gossip is the death of all good things in a team.

Do you remember playing telephone as a grade school kid? Me, too! It was always hilarious how messed up the words got as the secret went around the circle. My dance coach, Jen Phillips, used to have us play this game before performances. I thought it was because the game was fun. I now know there were two bigger reasons.

Numero uno: Dozens of little girls hopped up on nerves, makeup, and AquaNet are truly a force to be reckoned with. These little ladies must be contained pre-performance.

Numero dos: My coach was brilliant. She began teaching us at the earliest possible age that gossip sucks. No matter how carefully you whisper the secret to the girl sitting next to you, the message is going to get messed up. She used that game to teach us that the team cannot function and thrive when gossip is present. Jen loved us and dance so much that, years later, she took on the position of coaching the Payette Pi-Rettes with her bestie, Julie Dorman. I spent four years on a team of teenage girls watching masterful leadership in action. Gossip was squelched as it should be. If you were found to be involved in mean girl activities, there were penalties to pay. Because the precedent was set, we really didn't do it.

Consequently, we had an award-winning, butt-kicking team. We also had the time of our lives. To this day, I love my memories as a Pi-Rette and am thankful gossip was not allowed.

In short, your team is instrumental in the success of your hygiene program. Care well for it, and it will care well for you. Aaannnnnnd: don't gossip. 😉

Dear Jen and Julie,

If you ever read my dental geek book, know that I love you. I learned from you, and I'm teaching a no-gossip policy at every chance I get. I am also focusing on being a winner (#InsideJoke #PreperfomanceFun #DanceTeamRocks). Thank you for being such a critical part of the village that raised my teammates and me. You ladies are the beez kneez. ❤️

Love, Bran

Stellar Teamwork

1. List each teammate you have on the back side of this page using the table below to organize your answers.

2. In a round table discussion have each member of the team report their job description and special contributions to the function of the practice. Use this information to fill out the middle column next to each teammate's name.

3. Consider how your role on the team could incorporate actions to support each member of your team. Write this in the third column of your table.

4. Commit to your role as a supporting member for each of your teammates whole heartedly. Actively complete one task for each team member from the third column Every. Single. Day.

Follow these simple steps...

...and watch your team flourish! Joy and career satisfaction will skyrocket within your practice. Be sure to share your success with me and your other dental friends. Let's be the change we wish to see and the example we wish to set!

Stellar Outcomes

Brandi Hooker Evans, RDH-ER, MHE
(208) 244-2141 • BrandiHookerEvans.com
StellarOutcomes@outlook.com

Stellar Teamwork

Name:	Role in the practice & special contributions:	How you can support this teammate from your position:

Stellar Outcomes

Brandi Hooker Evans, RDH-ER, MHE
(208) 244-2141 • BrandiHookerEvans.com
StellarOutcomes@outlook.com

Chapter 11

The Freaking Finances

"**O**K, Gary, thanks for coming in today. I enjoyed our deep dive into your health through one of your most intimate orifices: your mouth. Now, this is the part of the appointment where I will get awkward and leave you hanging." I walk Gary to the front office, "Sally, Gary is all done for the day and is ready for you to go over his treatment plan and insurance. Oh, and can you schedule him back for scaling and root planing? Cool! Thanks, have a great day!" (Then I briskly walk down the hall to avoid *any and all* time and money conversations needed to complete Gary's initial stage of care.)

I jest. But—do I? Have you ever done or seen this?? I sure have. I used to believe that the front office rock stars were the experts on the schedule and money, so why mess up their flow? If this is you, I get it. It was me. *And* we can do better. By our team, by our patients, and by ourselves.

Spoiler alert! We are educated professionals licensed to provide care to other human beings. The knowledge, skills, education, products, and expertise needed take time and are worth compensation. Patients utilize their resources of time, energy, money, and dental insurance in exchange for these services we provide. The fact that you are still reading this book tells me you're ready to become more competent at having the time and money conversations.

The conversations might sound something like this:

"Gary, we will treat this gum disease in all four quarters of your mouth. Think of it like having one cavity in each area. Instead of fillings, we will remove the buildup and destroy the biofilm. Each area costs roughly $250. We'll complete what we call 'periodontal therapy' on the right side of your mouth today and schedule one and a half hours to take care of the left side of your mouth and polish all of your teeth ASAP. Let's match up our schedules. I have next Monday at 3:30 or Wednesday at noon. Does either of those work for you?"

Gary: "Lunchtime on Wednesday works for me. I have a health savings account. May I use that for this?"

Me: "Absolutely. When we finish up here, let's visit with Sally about how to make the financial part easy for you. Do you want to stick with lunchtime on Wednesdays for our three-month 'kick this disease's butt' appointments?"

Gary: "Sure thing."

Me: Schedule the scaling and root planing and one year of maintenance appointments for Gary right now.

Us: *Winning!*

Prices of scaling and root planing vary wildly. However, quadrants of 4341 are a very similar price to a two-surface filling in most practices. The direct comparison to having a cavity is one most people immediately understand. Sharing the specifics shows Gary that we know what we are talking about and that we do not take the commitment lightly. Allowing Sally to answer the more in-depth questions and come up with the plan allows each teammate to contribute their specialty. The alternative is to drop Gary off with Sally with no setup. That isn't nice or helpful. It also means that Gary will be less likely to work with us to heal his periodontal disease.

We can set expectations for years of excellent dental hygiene care by explaining, "Typically we take X-rays once a year, the doctor provides an exam twice yearly, and we meet for three-month periodontal maintenance visits. This recipe ensures that the destructive bacteria cannot repopulate and cause damage. We kick them out, and over time, the types of bacteria that can grow will evolve into a less dangerous set of strains! How freaking cool is that?!"

Before we move further into more sample conversations, I want to "press pause" and pose a few questions. Sit up tall, take a deep breath, and get ready to ponder the following:

- Do I believe scaling and root planing work?

- Do I believe the knowledge, skill, and expertise needed to complete scaling and root planing are different/more advanced than that of a prophy?

- Do I believe I am qualified to provide periodontal therapy?

❋ When considering the monetary price of scaling and root planing in my office, do I believe the health benefits are worth that cost?

❋ Do I believe the health implications of not treating periodontitis are severe?

❋ Do I believe that oral health and systemic health are intertwined, or are they not related?

These are not trick questions. I asked them because if our beliefs do not align with our values, we cannot proceed. As quality health care providers, we must believe in the worth of our services, and the profoundly positive effects said services will have on their health. Our patients, by the way, come to us knowing little to nothing about periodontology. They are frequently new to the "wellness" arena. Many of them believe that if something does not hurt, it cannot be a problem. When we converse without conviction that what we do works, that the health benefit is worth ten times the financial cost associated, our "case acceptance" is super low. This results in our patients continuing to live with disease.

Recently, I worked with a team where the dentist (I'll call him Ryan) asked if four-month recares would be sufficient for perio maintenance after scaling and root planing. Upon further discussion, we uncovered that Ryan was not convinced that three-month recares supported optimal patient health. He thought that was one more out-of-pocket cost for his patients. He believed that four-month visits were adequate. We examined the research together, and he noted that the bacterial biofilm becomes mature at twelve weeks, on average, and that leaving the destructive biofilm alone for an additional month was detrimental to the success of scaling and root planing as well as the patients' long-term, overall health. He also thought this counterproductive for their investment in initial therapy. Ryan is very passionate about providing quality care to his patients. He believes that the care he provides can change their lives—and I agree with him! After diving deeper into his belief system about cost and recares, we found the belief that was holding him back, and he let it go. Since then, Ryan's confidence in presenting the comprehensive care plan has skyrocketed. So has his care plan acceptance.

Bottom line: To adopt this style of care, we each must be able to look in the mirror and say, "My name is _____. I am a registered dental hygienist in the state of _____. I believe in nonsurgical periodontal therapy and the three-month periodontal maintenance formula for eliminating and/or controlling periodontal disease. I know that improved oral health is critical to overall health. I also know that untreated and poorly managed periodontal disease will cause catastrophic damage to my patients' bodies. As a clinician, I provide proficient dental hygiene services. These services are worth far more than my office charges for them."

If any of that makes you cringe, we need to dig deeper and find out what is causing the misalignment between beliefs and values. Go back to the six questions we discussed a few paragraphs ago and decide if you are ready to do everything it takes to answer in the affirmative. Alternatively, seek a different philosophy of care that aligns with your values and beliefs.

If, as you completed that statement, you thought, "Heck, yes! I totally agree! I love that it doesn't cost ten times as much, so even more people can commit to this awesome care I provide for their health!" Then rock on, friend. You are in the right place to participate in this version of dental care! Also, you may be a dental geek if you talk like that. Don't worry. I am too. 😉

Next sample conversation: Sheldon.

Sheldon has insurance, so we need to add a few key points to the financial conversation. "Sheldon, I'm so glad we're going to get to work on your healing. It looks like you have a dental benefit we should use as best we can! Now that we are treating disease rather than preventing it, this company (insert their insurance company) will view our plan the same as if there were a cavity in each quarter of your mouth. This means you have a deductible to meet and a copay for the care. Surely, Sally can share those specific numbers with you upfront. The other item worthy of note with your dental benefit is that they will likely help with two maintenances per year rather than the needed four."

Sheldon rolls his eyes. I say, "I agree. Dental insurance can be frustrating and wildly inadequate for basic dental needs of the average person. I promise you that we will do our best to maximize your benefit from them. The cost is minor when you look at the value of lifelong health. However, it can feel burdensome upfront. I will cuss them out with you until they catch up with what 'insurance' ought to be."

Sheldon might want to know more about the help that his insurance will provide. This can get super tricky because the insurance companies vary, and the plan the patient has within that company can also vary a lot. In this case, take Sheldon to a spot where he and Sally can sit down and review his policy privately. They will be able to come up with a quality plan. Great job doing your part in setting it up!

A word of caution to your peeps with dental insurance. Do not bill more than two quadrants in one day without written consent from the insurance provider. It is better to have them back another day for a fine scale and polish than to do the work for the full mouth and only get paid for half.

If Lily does not have insurance and comments that she is concerned about affording care, the conversation could go like this. "Lily, I am so happy we have the opportunity to treat this gum disease. You are going to feel great and enjoy the benefits forever. We have a few options to ensure you can get the care you need now. Sally is an expert in finding the best one for you. Let's go ask her to share them with us." Then Sally can go over the cash option and/or third-party financing. If we have already set up the financial conversation in the operatory, the investment will not be a shock to Lily. This evokes further trust in us as professionals, and Lily will be more likely to work with us to heal her periodontal disease.

In summary, the treatment of periodontal disease requires time, money, and effort by the patient and the practitioner. As the practitioner, we are responsible for having the knowledge, skills, and supplies to complete care. The patient is responsible for paying for said goods and services as well as their behavior between recare appointments. The exchange that occurs is like any other health care or business transaction. Consider this chapter our permission slip to feel fabulous about what we do and have high-quality conversations about all aspects of care with all our patients!

Hope

*L*et's work together. Let's reimagine how financing dental care could be. Let's create something that serves everyone well. What would it be like if we started having conversations like this:

To every single person with dental insurance,

Thank you for working hard to obtain an insurance benefit. Whether your company pays for it as part of your compensation package, you buy it privately, or a family member provides it for you, I applaud the effort it takes to acquire dental insurance. Truly, this is a fantastic feat.

It is with deep regret that I inform you this insurance is likely nothing of what you hope for. It will likely let you and your dentist down time and time again. If you find yourself needing dental care, the chances of your "insurance" ensuring that you get the necessary care at a fair cost is almost nonexistent.

The idea of what dental insurance *should* be is beautiful. Unfortunately, unless all you need are preventive cleanings twice a year, you will find yourself without "coverage." However, there has never been a better time to speak up for a positive change.

I would encourage you to write a letter to your insurance company about what you hope dental insurance would help you with. Share with them your personal situation and dental struggles. Let them know you hope they would compensate the dental business you seek care at. Tell them you appreciate the assistance they provide. Discuss that the current rate of care denial and maximum benefit are inadequate for the care you need. I advise you to be kind yet firm about what you need if you are going to continue to support their company with your premiums.

It would also be wise to consider starting a dental savings account. Save your premiums and pay cash for the care you need. The beauty of using your own money is that your deductible will never start over, your benefit will never go unclaimed, your care will never be denied, your maximum will never be met, and your dentist never not paid. I realize this is a contrary concept to the "insurance" we have come to believe we need. However, the "insurance" we "need" isn't ensuring much peace of mind or quality dental care.

In short, you have the ability to advocate for yourself. Your health and wellness are worth it. I am on your team and doing everything I can to pave a new path for us all.

In the meantime, do not count on the insurance company to know what you need. Rather, find a dentist and their team that you trust. Learn how to recognize health and disease in your own body and let the team you trust help you achieve your best outcome.

Sincerely,

Your hygienist pal, Brandi

––––––––––––––––––––

Dear administrative team in charge of all things insurance,

Thank you for your amazing dedication to such a frustrating task! The unending mess that the insurance companies have created for you and the practices you serve is abysmal. Your hard work and dedication are admirable; we all appreciate you immensely.

Please don't give up. Please keep submitting and resubmitting periodontal charts, X-rays, clinic notes, and narratives. Please keep highlighting the information missed by the insurance "dental experts." Please don't lose hope. Please know that your hard work today creates evidence that will serve our tomorrows. You are helping us show that we will not stand for the insurance companies dictating dental care any longer.

Please feel encouraged and refreshed by this letter. You are making a positive difference. Even though it feels like it doesn't matter, it does. Every single step you take to right this wrong is causing a ripple effect that will help the patients and the teams that serve them in the future.

In the meantime, call me if you need to cuss. I so get it and am writing the same denial argument letters with you. I am winning some cases and losing some. Together, we are going to make this better. We will advocate for one patient at a time. It is the right thing to do, and please don't ever stop.

With gratitude,

Brandi

———————————

Dear president of all insurance companies,

Good afternoon. Thank you for taking the time to consider working together for a brighter future. I believe that, together, we can craft a plan that takes excellent care of you, your employees, your clients, and your dental providers.

As you know, disease is rampant in our nation. Between caries and periodontal disease, more than half of our population is negatively affected by dental ailments.[9] Many of these people are clients of yours. They often find themselves without adequate assistance in the dental office when their disease is diagnosed and needs treatment. This is upsetting to them because they have paid for "insurance." It is also contrary to your mission as a caring company that wants to aid in the eradication of dental disease whenever possible.

Because you exist to serve people and their dental needs, we will assess the current and projected needs of the population you insure. We can create an initiative that supports prevention, which is always less expensive than treatment. In addition, our collaboration can aim to adjust reimbursement rates to be consistent with the cost of providing care. It would also be beneficial to negotiate a maximum benefit that supports patients' ability to complete the care they need. We can compile a complete list and begin working to accomplish goals immediately.

Doing right by your clients will bring success to your business. The financial reward for efficiently serving your mission will be robust. The delight in being truly benevolent will increase your career satisfaction and enjoyment as well as the loyalty of your employees. This will be a fulfilling, purpose-driven mission that will make the world a better place. Thank you in advance for your dedication and partnership.

Let's find a time to meet and discuss the mission of your insurance company and how we can best achieve those goals.

Optimistically yours,

Brandi

(Notice that I did *not* cuss them out and call them names. They have done many wrongs, but focusing on the past will only bring more discord. Cussing one another out will get us nowhere. These insurance companies have all the money, all the lobbying power, and all the ability to be a part of positive change. We *must* appeal to their humanity. The CEO, president, representatives, and call center team members are *humans*. They want to have purpose and make a positive impact on this world. They are running a business and must know they will still be financially rewarded when they do the right thing. It is a change we have to start. So, right here. You and me. Let's be kind in the present and build the brightest future).

What can you do to be a part of the change for the better?

Chapter 12

Care For The Whole, Not Just The Hole

*H*ere's the thing, Hygiene Team: now, more than ever before, our patients need us. And sadly, our picking and scratching ain't gonna do the whole trick. Don't get me wrong, hand scaling, polishing, and (my personal favorite) ultrasonic-ing is *super* important. But superb plaque and calculus removal simply isn't enough.

We will have to dig deeper (instrumentation pun intended) if we want to make a true impact and help our patients finally get healthy. For the first time in history, more people are dying from chronic rather than communicable diseases.[10] We will have some fun sorting through some statistics, diseases, and strategies in this chapter. Many of us have firsthand experience with this, so be sure to make notes of your experiences and send them to me; I will share them!

What is your favorite, a sunrise or a sunset? Typically, when I ask this question, most people raise their hands to support sunsets.

My personal favorite is a sunrise. I love the quiet beginning of the day before the majority of souls have risen.

My question for you is: Which comes first? The sunrise or the sunset? Because you cannot have a sunrise without a sunset, and you cannot have a sunset without a sunrise. This is the same with our bodies and our mouths. There is no "what comes first;" they are a package deal, my friends! Buckle up for a bit of research.

"Many recent studies explore the interrelationship between oral health, inflammation, and systemic disease. Oral microbiota can cause oral inflammation but may also directly contribute to systemic inflammation, increasing inflammation through the release of toxins or leakage of microbial products into the bloodstream. The association between oral inflammation and systemic inflammation is fundamental to understanding the detrimental effects of oral inflammation on several organ systems and the ability of oral disease to increase the risk of developing non-oral disease."[11]

The point I am trying to make is that we have an interconnected, bidirectional relationship between oral health and systemic health. The secret is that there is no such thing as this or that health. #EveryHealthIsConnected

I am delighted to share a little snack of information about some emerging research that *Is So Exciting!* And super close to my heart. Previously, we had all been under the assumption that Alzheimer's disease and dementia are genetic and there is nothing you can do about them. Once you get it, you have it, and it progresses in the same way your granddad's did, and that is that. Well, thank goodness there are some fabulous, geeky, and smart scientists, researchers, and doctors out there who said, "That answer doesn't work for me. What else is there?"

What did they find? Drum roll, please. Alzheimer's and dementia are largely inflammatory-based diseases that are directly affected by *lifestyle*. So, yes, your patients' gum disease (aka inflammatory disease) puts them at risk for struggling with these no-good, very bad brain diseases also. Remember, every health is connected.

In 2014, I moved to Boise to help care for my Grandpa Hooker at the end of his life. Of all his health struggles in those last couple of years, Alzheimer's disease was the most heartbreaking for me to watch. I remember one morning, I was traveling from Ontario to Pocatello and stopped at my grandparents' house on the way. It was early. He was surprised to see me. In the span of about thirty minutes, we had the conversation, "Hi Dolly!! Where did you come from so early?!" nine times. By the way, Dolly is the nickname he gave me as a wee lass. To date, it is still my favorite name to be called. 💖

I happily repeated my response nine times, telling God that I would do the "Dolly, where did you come from?" conversation as many times as he wanted, as long as he knew I was Dolly. #Grateful

Scientists, researchers, and doctors have amazing news for us! Below are a few quick and simple ways to keep Gramps (and ourselves) remembering that I am Dolly:

- ⚬ Plenty of water.

- ⚬ Healthy fats rock—especially fish and olive oils!

☀ Dark leafy greens and berries are for eating. Daily.

☀ Time-reduced feeding (getting all your food for the day within a ten- to twelve-hour timeframe) is great for the brain.

☀ Move that bod—all the time!

☀ Challenge and stimulate your thinking self.

☀ Sleep well.

These are in no order, but they are a great start to a brighter future for us all. Also, shockingly, the rest of our *total health* will improve with these additions.

Many incredible resources are available if you want to learn more about this disease and its prevention/reversal. I have several favorites, but honestly, you can do an internet search for "Alzheimer's prevention" and find a wealth of legitimate resources.[12]

I have a specially dedicated place in my heart for Alzheimer's patients and their families, so don't hesitate to reach out if you want to chat.

About autoimmune diseases in general—did you know that up to 23.5 million Americans have an autoimmune disease?[13] Many of which the first manifestations occur in the oral cavity. AND if caught and diagnosed early, the treatment effectiveness and quality of life improve exponentially! Hello, oral cancer screening! Thank you for your information.

Early detection of any of these diseases just changed a person's life forever. I went back to the Mayo Clinic for information on managing all these diseases. There was a wide range of treatment modalities and medications. Still, for every single disease, the common recommendations were basic anti-inflammatory items such as: rest, exercise, stress reduction, and anti-inflammatory food (fruits and veggies, omega-3 fatty acids, and vitamin D).

Let's look at a few of the typical diseases we see regularly.

Sjögren's syndrome is a common autoimmune rheumatic disease. The symptoms experienced the most often are extreme fatigue, dry eyes, and dry mouth (xerostomia). The latter can ultimately result in swallowing difficulties, progressive and severe tooth decay, and oral infections. Even if the patient carries out excellent oral hygiene, they may experience high numbers of dental caries and tooth loss. No cure currently exists for Sjögren's syndrome.

Saliva composition can also be affected by aging; dry mouth in elderly patients is often caused by anticholinergic medications.[14]

What effective modalities against dry mouth have you had good luck with? My favorite recommendation is to add milk (of any kind) to a meal. The fat in the milk provides lubrication for mastication. This is a simple, cheap, and easy (my kind of addition 😉) way to mitigate the undesirable effects of xerostomia. All joking aside, if our patients cannot eat comfortably or at all, the ability to support their immune system is drastically reduced. Anything we can do to help them fuel their bodies with nutrients is worth doing.

Let's take a peek at the *thyroid gland*. The thyroid is the prime regulator of metabolism and has an impact on all the functions of the body. If the thyroid operates too much or too little, it can adversely affect any part of the body.[15] Should our patient be on medication, appropriate risk management must occur. Several times a year, every year since 2007, I have recommended a patient get their thyroid checked out. In that time, not even one person was upset with me for being thorough. We wish that thyroid disorders were not a thing. Since they are, this is an excellent opportunity to refer people to and work with endocrinologists. Let the collaboration and knowledge-gaining commence!

How about that red butterfly patch denoting Lupus on John? Did you know lupus fluctuates as much as any disease based on lifestyle choices?[16] Warding off, struggling, or thriving despite lupus is largely in the hands of the individual. According to the Mayo Clinic, if caught early, treatment is much more effective for lupus. While not curable, medications such as nonsteroidal anti-inflammatory drugs, corticosteroids, antimalarial drugs, immunosuppressants, and biologics can all help manage the autoimmune disease and prolong the quality and quantity of life for the patient. We are lucky to have these options when salads and walks aren't enough.

As if the pain and hindrance of dang *rheumatoid arthritis* weren't enough, check out this nugget from a research article: "A number of oral manifestations have been described in rheumatoid arthritis patients. These include the well-recognized association with Sjogren's and xerostomia, TMD, methotrexate-induced ulcers, and an increasing emphasis on periodontal disease. Oral mucosal involvement in autoimmune diseases, including rheumatoid arthritis, occurs with high frequency. Symptomatic xerostomia and secondary Sjogren's are not uncommon in rheumatoid arthritis patients, with recent studies providing prevalence estimates of between 3 and 30%, depending on the definition."[17]

Moving further south. The CDC reported that in 2015–2016, 3.1 million American adults had been diagnosed as having an *inflammatory bowel disease (IBD)*.[18] This means that a significant portion of our population cannot absorb and assimilate food correctly. They end up with a situation called "leaky gut," which makes them more susceptible to diseases of every kind. It also prevents the critical nutrients in the food from being used in the body.[19] It is a vicious cycle that controls daily life.

As someone who has struggled with IBS for more than a decade, I can attest to the fact that this is miserable. It is impossible to be well when you have a constant stomachache. The good thing about IBD is that, usually, diet and good stress-handling skills can control the symptoms. Happily, I am celebrating fourteen years without IBS. That disease that "has no cure" and will require "prescription-strength medicine" is all healed up for me. If you or your patients struggle in this arena, let's chat. There are many paths to healing. Often, signs of inflammation occur in the mouth as *unexplained redness of the tissues or mouth sores.* If one of your patients exhibits any of these symptoms, having a conversation with them about their stomach health would be pertinent. Bottom line: we are early detectors!

How about the fact that research is now getting brave enough to say there is a casual relationship between periodontitis and heart disease? The verbiage is getting firmer because the evidence is outstanding.[20] Every year, we lose almost 700,000 Americans to heart disease—the number one cause of death[21]—and another

160,000 to stroke.[22] My friends, are we feeling called to action yet?!?!?!?!?!?!?! Our bodies are connected from head to toe, or "stem to stern," to quote my mom.

If the number one killer of Americans is exacerbated by infection in the mouth, then it is our responsibility to address this crisis as such. The other day, I heard a dentist say (while his hygienist confirmed), "It's just gum disease. It's not like we are fighting cancer or anything as serious as that." I sat silent and blinked my eyes because, as best as I can tell, if potentially mitigating the effects of the number one killer of Americans isn't serious, I don't know what is.

How about those poor, unfortunate livers? Liver disease is another chronic condition that is greatly affected by periodontitis.[23] Perio puts a severe tax on the liver. The liver spies the invaders and responds by releasing cytokines and LDLs into the bloodstream.[24] Not ideal. We are seeing more non-alcoholic fatty liver disease (NAFDL) than ever before.[25] NAFDL is a hepatic manifestation of metabolic syndrome.[26] As we need our livers to filter chemicals in our blood, I think it best not to add to its grief with unnecessary periodontal disease.

Does anyone have middle schoolers in here? They have an uncanny ability to find the one inappropriate thing about any situation and then bust up laughing until they can't breathe or even tell you what was so funny. Since I have raised four, I can say that their ability for crass humor is stupendous. One day, when I was working on this section for a presentation, they picked up on a medical history question I was working on regarding genital herpes. After loud laughter and a sex talk with their mother (that they didn't want to have), they left the conversation knowing how herpes spreads from human to human and place to place on the body. 🤣 Sweaty as that conversation with my kids was, we must also be professionals and examine all aspects of the health history.

According to the CDC, more than 12 percent of Americans have genital herpes.[27] This is important to note because oral herpes (what we see is caused by HSV-1) can be spread to the genitals through oral sex. If a patient marks "yes" on cold sores and fever blisters, it is worth having a conversation about how the virus spreads. I am not suggesting you give the sex talk like I did with my kids, but a quick question about their knowledge about how an open lesion is contagious is worthy fodder for the dental appointment. #AwkwardTopic #MovingOn

On to *diabetes*, periodontal disease behaves in the same manner as cardiovascular disease and other inflammatory diseases. It has long been known that periodontal disease and diabetes are interconnected.[28] The take-home message in this section is to support our patients with either of these diseases in a more profound manner. Finger-wagging about A1C levels and home care isn't going to cut the mustard. We must start having profound conversations about mitigating blood sugar spikes with easy and fun lifestyle recommendations.

Here are some patient conversation ideas: Tell your diabetic pal Hal that working out first thing in the morning can help his blood sugar levels stabilize for the whole day. Tell Hal that having a savory breakfast after his workout is an excellent way to set the stage for his body to function well all day long. Encourage him to eat vegetables or nuts at the beginning of every meal and snack to avoid blood sugar spikes at eating times.

People who are struggling with diabetes are often frustrated about how hard it is to manage the disease in our current culture of eat-refined-carbohydrates-all-day-everyday and the constant temptation to sit and scroll.

Whew. That was a lot of info!! Thanks for hanging in there with me.

How many of you have one of these diseases or know someone who does? What if we could love them better by helping them reduce the risk or severity of any one of these diseases? The *health hack* is to eliminate the source of chronic inflammation!!

Periodontal disease hinders the immune system by helping cause other diseases. Disease in any system in the body hinders the immune system, thus exacerbating periodontal disease. It's a two-way street, my friends!

According to the CDC, 65.5 percent of Americans see their dentist once a year, while only 30 percent see their physician.[29] At the dental office, 90 percent of patients spend approximately 90 percent of their time with hygienists. That means we are the health care professionals with the most time with our captive audience. Let's captivate them with valuable information and fill them up with love!

When we lecture our patients from the podium, they disengage. What do you think they are noticing about our faces? Perhaps a zit or a sunmark. Maybe a booger, no, wait—we have a mask on, so maybe a sleepy crust in the eye. You get the point. They are not listening to a lecture. They realize the dental light has streaks on it and wonder if that is from someone else's spit. 😌

Remember, build a strong case and let the patient tell *you* they have gum disease (or cavities), not the other way around. Follow their discovery with fun, easy ways to reduce inflammation in their lives. Your connection, rapport, and delight in being a dental hygienist will flourish immensely.

Next are a few of my favorite "whole body" conversations to have with patients:

- ☀ What habits are you proud of? Big or small.

- ☀ When was the last time you had a good laugh? If you want, I'll tell you some fun facts about laughter (insert things like it boosts the immune system, protects us from infections, releases endorphins in our brains, reduces stress hormones such as cortisol, reduces blood pressure, and increases circulation). Or you can ditch the long list and just find something to laugh about together!

- ☀ How do you connect with people and things that bring you joy?

- ☀ Did you know you can support your immune system (and your mind) by simply taking a walk? Who is your favorite person to chat with? Perhaps they could join you in person or via the telephone?

- ☀ My favorite convo with anyone who will engage is around nutrition. I like: "Because gum disease is an immune response, we can help you live a healthier life by finding foods that boost your immune system." My favorite game to play is 'Find the Veggie!' Did you know that if you order a salad instead of a burrito at Costa Vida, you get everything you wanted in your burrito *plus* two cups of leafy greens? It's the same price and way more fun to eat. Watch out, though. There is a lie floating around that adding veggies is expensive. Don't let that suck you in. A basket full of produce is less than half the price of premade foods, and anything you don't use up can be frozen and added to a smoothie when you're in a hurry and have to take a meal on the go!" (Obviously, that was the extended version, but you get the point.)

Want to try this next time you're in the op? Pick a point of conversation, then *wait* and *listen*. Participate and celebrate whatever they come up with!

Most people already know that brushing and flossing is the answer to their plaque problem, so let's surprise them by dropping the subject and talking about other systems of the body. *This* is where we can truly move the needle.

Remember earlier when we discussed that our amazing plaque and calculus removal isn't enough? Here, it is in the thick of what we do. It is time to *move on* from finger-wagging and browbeating our patients to try to get them to floss, and it is time to start getting excited about dropping juicy conversation bombs like the ones above. Those chats lead to them committing to care in the office *and* stopping at the grocery store on the way home for that power toothbrush that they know they need (wink, wink—

we recommended they get that six months ago, but because we are operating at this new advanced level, we don't even have to mention it today).

At the end of the day, we are the bridge between oral and total body health. We are trusted, educated, and equipped to be the change we wish to see. Our patients, their smiles, and the health of our population are counting on us to step up and lead the way to a healthier future. This is our chance to be the *Thing* that made a difference. Let's not wait one more minute. Sweeping disease under the rug is not serving any of us. Together, you and me, let's be the Thing—one *whole* patient at a time.

What will you take with you to your clinical conversations?

Chapter 13

Abstinence

*H*ey, now, get your mind out of the gutter. Just because I'm a "Hooker" doesn't mean we're talking about that type of abstinence. JK. You do your personal life. I'm here to discuss why you or anyone would abstain from changing how they show up in the dental world.

There is always the problem of the learning curve. Trying something new takes practice and is uncomfortable until you get the hang of it. You might stumble over some words or feel vulnerable during your transition.

It would also make sense to pass on proactive hygiene appointments if you believe oral health is not modifiable with the care and education we provide.

No one would blame you for skipping individualized care if working as a dental professional was simply a means to an end to acquire a paycheck.

Perhaps you have been practicing for decades and believe feeling energized about your career is a lost cause.

Big, deep breath in—hold, two, three, four. Slowly let it out, two, three, four.

"It's our light, not our darkness, that most frightens us." Marianne Williamson penned that juicy little wisdom nugget, and I believe she is right. We are *full* of light and can make a tremendously positive difference.

In my opinion, the crux of the issue is that we are scared of the idea that we may have the power to affect our patients' lives profoundly. If we have this power, then the responsibility is large. We are so much more than "teeth cleaners," which feels weighty. In our culture, we are told to dream big and taught to play small. I challenge myself and everyone whose eyeballs are reading this to let go of playing small.

We health care providers have the ability and the opportunity to change the world!! Every time we positively impact the health and wellness of a human being who walks into our space, we have made the world a better place. Each time we value autonomy and empower our patients to become the stewards of their own health, the entire community is strengthened and blessed.

I hope and pray that we all will seek the courage to step into our potential as vessels for change and become the prevention specialists we are qualified to be. Step into the periodontal disease a$$-kicker role because we will change the world alone (and together). #OneHumanAtATime

Might I qualify that I've shared the philosophy of dental hygiene care that I have found to be successful for myself and many others? This does not mean it is the only way. I invite you to try all of it wholeheartedly and improve upon it. Use the pieces and parts that work well for you and scrap those that don't. The key points are:

1. Ditch the dental Greek lingo.

2. Don't be a donkey; do the assessment.

3. Shush! Let them tell you they have perio.

4. Offer all the options for care.

5. Love them where they're at, even if they aren't ready to proceed.

6. Diagnose disease; don't worry about the bottom line.

7. Compare notes with your team and keep practicing.

8. Be your best as a stellar clinician.

9. Keep those recares close.

10. The team is everything.

11. Talk about finances early and in the operatory.

12. Care well for the "whole" human.

Please use this page to journal any and all thoughts you have about this style of care. Or draw a cute cow picture and daydream about how much more fulfilling patient interactions are going to be. 💖

Yeehaw!

*D*ear dentists, hygienists, and cows who have read up to this point,

As you proceed forward, I am cheering you on. I pray for you, your patients, and your practice health and wellness. Thank you for taking your precious time to join me on this journey away from herding cattle and into providing exquisite, individualized care to every patient lucky enough to sit in your operatory.

Cheers to the next chapter in our careers.

Lovingly yours,

Brandi

Acknowledgments

Grateful does not begin to cover it when I think about how blessed I am. Along the way, I am particularly grateful for my parents and family: Clay, Marshell, Kathleen and Rob. They taught me how to love and celebrate no matter what. How to find the good in any circumstance because failures and misfortunes have their benefits, too. Sometimes, it takes a while to figure out the benefits, but they do show up—eventually!

Piper, Summer, Violet, Kyler, and Moon: I love you more than words can express. Our little family is the center of my heart. Know that I am one million percent in each of your corners.

My darling husband and fellow dental geek Eron: thank you for being with me since it was "Hooker's Hygiene." I am so happy to have shared the gathering, dreaming, executing, and never-ending growing seasons with you. I love our life together and, of course, our gram-negative pillow talk. 😘

A big fat thank you to my brother Luke. Your support and friendship are priceless. Thanks for being one of the few who knows just how goofy I really am. And thanks for believing in me since the beginning of time.

To my best good best ~Janica~ Sis, we have done all the things together: became RDHs, wives, moms, survived devastation, celebrated wins big and small, cried for all the reasons, and the list goes on. I simply could not do it without you.

I would also love to thank my first editor and clarifier Mrs. Lori Bulloch. Girl, you get me, and this book is so blessed to have had your caring heart, hands, and prayers upon it! Your guidance on where to add and where to cut has been invaluable. *And* your friendship means the world to me.

Thank you to the best instructors and classmates a girl could dream up. Idaho State University class and faculty of 2007, you are forever in my heart and at the top of my gratitude list.

To my friends, colleagues, and patients, I learn from you daily and am endlessly cheering for your wellness. I hope you know I love to be in your presence. I also hope this work brings goodness to your life as you have brought so much to mine. Sam, you are at the top of this list. 💋

I would also like to thank every single rough experience, unkind critic, and tough patch in my life. I have learned, benefitted, and grown from each of you as much, if not more than anything. I hope I continue to get better at meeting you with *grace*.

A thank you opportunity would not be complete without the top of my list being noted. God, I am grateful for You. I appreciate the faith You have given me. Please continue to bless my thoughts, words, and actions to bring forth love and light.

To the team at Indie Books International, thank you so much for bringing this book to life. You took my vision and made it even more professional and lovely than I had hoped. Thank you for this gift.

How these parts of books aren't seventy pages long is a mystery to me. I feel like I want to thank my thankfulness. 😂 I will stop here, but if you are reading this, know that I had to try really hard to keep it concise.

About The Author

*B*randi has a ministry of joy. You can find her creating delicious food, finding fun (and sun) outdoors, and traveling the world. Recently, she added rest to her repertoire and covets time on her front porch with a glass of sparkling wine or water in hand. She highly recommends you take a time out to try it at your place or stop by hers. 😉 Brandi is an international speaker and published author passionate about turning science into action. Audiences are captivated by her engaging courses, leaving them inspired and equipped with valuable tools to provide exquisite, individualized care and lead a truly fulfilling life. Brandi acquired her formal education from Idaho State University, most recently, a master's degree in health education. Brandi has served the Idaho Dental Hygienists' Association as President and her local Portneuf Valley Dental Hygiene Society.

She has enjoyed nearly two decades as a clinician in private practice. Brandi treasured her time as a clinical dental hygiene faculty at Idaho State University and served on the ISU Dental Hygiene Advisory Board. Currently, Brandi owns and operates

Stellar Outcomes and Evans Dental with her husband, Dr. Eron Evans. Brandi is an American Academy of Dental Hygiene accredited continuing education provider. Brandi's passion for her craft translates into highly educational, motivational, and enjoyable experiences. She specializes in crafting tailored practice improvement programs, seamlessly integrating restorative and administrative insights to elevate individual dental offices and captivate large speaking audiences alike.

Brandi believes our time on earth is a precious gift. She intends to learn as much as possible while adding joy wherever she goes. Have a peek at what she is up to at www.BrandiHookerEvans.com.

Auto Note Example:

Doctor:

Registered Dental Hygienist:

Arrival:

Hygiene services provided today:

Chief Concerns:

Health History Updates:

Blood Pressure:

Oral Cancer Screening:

X-rays:

Plaque level:

Calculus located:

Periodontal Status:

Periodontal Classification:

Risk Factors:

Location of Sensitivity:

Anesthetic:

Treatment:

Hygiene Instruction:

Patient Interests:

Treatment Plan Options:

Treatment Plan Acceptance:

Next Visit:

"How to" spend the appointment in health.

When health is not present, more time will be needed.

First 20:
- ⁂ Medical history update
- ⁂ Wash hands
- ⁂ Blood pressure
- ⁂ Oral Cancer screening
- ⁂ Radiographs & intraoral pictures
- ⁂ Full mouth perio probe update

Next 25:
- ⁂ Ultra-sonic instrumentation
- ⁂ Hand instrumentation
- ⁂ Floss
- ⁂ Polish

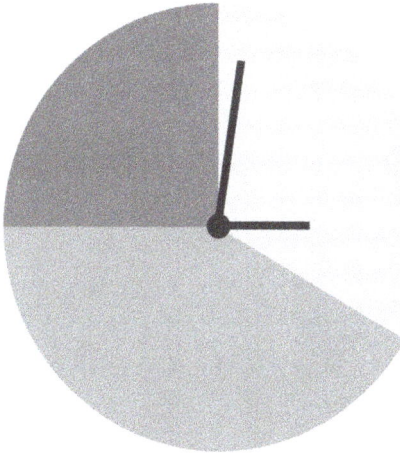

Last 15:
- ⁂ Exam with Doctor (Best to accommodate anytime based on availability)
- ⁂ Schedule next appointment
- ⁂ Answer any questions
- ⁂ Fabulous walk out and hand off to administrative staff

Begin to get your team on your level.
Simply tear this page out and discuss over burritos
with your teammates!
Be sure to invite everyone.

Radiographic Review

Radiographs are an essential piece to the assessment puzzle. For periodontal disease, x-rays are the key determining factor between preventive and treatment needs. It is of paramount importance to acquire diagnostic films. Once radiographs have been obtained, the clinician must be able to scrutinize the pictures for disease indicators as well as effectively present the conditions to the patient.

In Health:

- The thick white line should go up, over, and down
- PDL follows root of tooth in uniform size
- Crestal bone presents as thick white casing starting adjacent to the PDL and crossing the interproximal space between teeth
- Bone is 1-1.5 mm apical to the CEJ

The earliest changes should be noted and discussed with each patient. Permanent damage is imminent should the changes not be treated upon discovery. It is estimated that 30 to 50 percent of the bone has resorbed when radiographically visible. Inflammation of the periodontal ligament and crestal bone density may be restored with proper treatment and maintenance. Once bone height has been compromised the destruction is permanent: complete health cannot be restored.

Catching and treating periodontitis early is the difference our patients need care providers to make in their long-term health. Once proper homecare has been established and professional intervention has taken place, the bacterial bio-film can shift composition and become less virulent.

Presenting to the Patient:

Review immune response

☼ Our bodies will fight the infection. After a period of time, depending on our individual immune system, our bodies will try to get away from the infection. This presents as inflamed PDLs and bone shrinking away.

Review what the periodontal ligament should look like

☼ Uniform black line surrounding each tooth

Review what the bone should look like

☼ Thick white shell surrounds the tooth's PDL then connecting the adjacent tooth

☼ 1-1.5 mm below the CEJ

Call attention to changes

☼ Have patient show us each area of radiographic involvement.

☼ Let the patient guide us through the findings whenever possible. Use the periodontal assessment chart to evaluate radiographs.

Appendix D

Endnotes

[1] P. I. Eke, B. A. Dye, L. Wei, G. O. Thornton-Evans, and R. J. Genco, "Prevalence of Periodontitis in Adults in the United States: 2009 and 2010," *Journal of Dental Research* 91, no. 10 (October 2012), (published online August 2012,) https://doi.org/10.1177/0022034512457373.

[2] Taylor Swift, vocalist, "Anti-Hero," by Taylor Swift and Jack Antonoff, track 3 on *Midnights*, Republic, 2022.

[3] American Thyroid Association, General Information/Press Room, accessed November 26, 2023, https://www.thyroid.org/media-main/press-room/.

[4] "Latest Pet Ownership and Spending Data from APPA Reveals Continued Strength of National Pet Industry in the Face of Economic Uncertainty," American Pet Products Association, March 23, 2023, https://www.americanpetproducts.org/news/press-release/latest-pet-ownership-and-spending-data-from-appa-reveals-continued-strength-of-national-pet-industry-in-the-face-of-economic-uncertainty, and "National Pet Industry Exceeds $123 Billion in Sales and Sets New Benchmark," American Pet Products Association, April 19, 2022, https://www.americanpetproducts.org/news/press-release/national-pet-industry-exceeds-$123-billion-in-sales-and-sets-new-benchmark.

[5] Michelle Megna, "Pet Ownership Statistics 2023," *Forbes*, updated June 21, 2023, https://www.forbes.com/advisor/pet-insurance/pet-ownership-statistics/#sources_section.

[6] Sixpence None the Richer, "Kiss Me," by Matt Slocum, track 4 on *Sixpence None the Richer*, Elektra, 1997.

[7] W. Johnston, G. Ramage, M. Paterson, J. L. Brown, D. MacKenzie, and S. Culshaw, "Investigating the Effects of Instrumentation on In Vitro Periodontitis Biofilms," Oral Sciences, University of Glasgow and NHS Greater Glasgow and Clyde, Scotland, UK.

[8] Peter L. Harrison and Rodrigo Neiva, "Nonsurgical Instrumentation: An Update," *Inside Dentistry* 10, no. 5 (May 2014), https://www.aegisdentalnetwork.com/id/2014/05/ nonsurgical-instrumentation-an-update.

[9] Eke, Dye, "Prevalence of Periodontitis in Adults in the United States, 2009 and 2010", *Journal of Dental Research*, Op.cit.

[10] Leigh Shaw-Taylor, "An Introduction to the History of Infectious Diseases, Epidemics and the Early Phases of the Long-Run Decline in Mortality," *The Economic History Review* 73, no. 3 (2020), doi:10.1111/ehr.13019.

[11] Fiona Q. Bui, Cassio Luiz Coutinho Almeida-da-Silva, Brandon Huynh, Alston Trinh, Jessica Liu, Jacob Woodward, Homer Asadi, and David M. Ojcius, "Association between Periodontal Pathogens and Systemic Disease," Biomedical Journal 42, no. 1 (February 2019), https://doi.org/10.1016/j.bj.2018.12.001.

[12] I love Dr. Dale Bredesen's work at https://www.apollohealthco.com.

[13] "Progress in Autoimmune Disease Research," National Institutes of Health, March 2005, https://www.niaid.nih.gov/sites/default/ files/adccfinal.pdf.

[14] S. A. Mathews et al., "Oral Manifestations of Sjögren's Syndrome," *Journal of Dental Research* 87, no. 4 (2008), doi:10.1177/154405910808700411.

[15] Shalu Chandna and Manish Bathla, "Oral Manifestations of Thyroid Disorders and its Management," *Indian Journal of Endocrinology and Metabolism* 15, supplement 2 (2011), doi:10.4103/2230-8210.83343.

[16] Mayo Clinic, "Lupus - Diagnosis and Treatment" Accessed December 14, 2023, https://www.mayoclinic.org/diseases-conditions/lupus/diagnosis-treatment/drc-20365790

[17] Clifton O. Bingham III and Malini Moni, "Periodontal Disease and Rheumatoid Arthritis: The Evidence Accumulates for Complex Pathobiologic Interactions," *Current Opinion in Rheumatology* 25, no. 3 (2013), doi:10.1097/BOR.0b013e32835fb8ec.

[18] E. P. Terlizzi, J. M. Dahlhamer, F. Xu, A. G. Wheaton, and K. J. Greenlund, "Health Care Utilization among U.S. Adults with Inflammatory Bowel Disease, 2015–2016," National Health Statistics Reports no. 152 (February 24, 2021), https://doi.org/10.15620/cdc:100471.

[19] Qinghui Mu, Jay Kirby, Christopher M. Reilly, and Xin M. Luo, "Leaky Gut As a Danger Signal for Autoimmune Diseases," *Front Immunol*, May 23, 2017, https://pubmed.ncbi.nlm.nih.gov/28588585/

[20] P. Hengjeerajaras, KY Liu, P. Maketone, V. Patel, Y. Shi, "The Link Between Periodontitis/Peri-implantis and Cardiovascular Disease,' .*Int J Periodontics Restorative Dental*,. Nov/Dec 2020, https://pubmed.ncbi.nlm.nih.gov/33151189/

[21] "Heart Disease," Centers for Disease Control, National Center for Health Statistics, last reviewed September 15, 2023, https://www.cdc.gov/nchs/fastats/heart-disease.htm.

[22] "Cerebrovascular Disease or Stroke," Centers for Disease Control, National Center for Health Statistics, last reviewed September 14, 2023, https://www.cdc.gov/nchs/fastats/stroke.htm.

[23] Goran Rinčić et al., "Association between Periodontitis and Liver Disease," *Acta Clinica Croatica* 60, no. 3 (2022), doi:10.20471/acc.2021.60.03.22.

[24] P. Han, D. Sun, J. Yang, "Interaction between periodontitis and liver diseases," *Biomed Rep.* September 5, 2016, https://pubmed. ncbi.nlm.nih.gov/27588170/

[25] R. Kuraji, S. Sekino, Y. Kapila, Y. Numabe, "Periodontal disease-related nonalcoholic fatty liver disease and nonalcoholic steatohepatitis: An emerging concept of oral-liver axis," *Periodontol 2000.* October 2021 https://pubmed.ncbi.nlm.nih. gov/34463983/

[26] Ryutaro Kuraji, Satoshi Sekino , Yvonne Kapila , Yukihiro Numabe, "Periodontal disease-related nonalcoholic fatty liver disease and nonalcoholic steatohepatitis: An emerging concept of oral-liver axis," *Periodontal 2000*, October 2021, https://pubmed. ncbi.nlm.nih.gov/34463983/

[27] Genital Herpes—CDC Detailed Fact Sheet, Centers for Disease Control and Prevention, last reviewed July 21, 2021 (archived document), https://www.cdc.gov/std/herpes/stdfact-herpes-detailed.htm.

[28] "Diabetes: Key Points," American Dental Association, last updated January 24, 2022, https://www.ada.org/resources/ research/science-and-research-institute/oral-health-topics/ diabetes.

[29] A.E. Cha, R.A. Cohen, "Urban-rural differences in dental care use among adults aged 18–64." *NCHS Data Brief*, no 412. (Hyattsville, MD: National Center for Health Statistics. 2021). https://www.cdc.gov/nchs/products/databriefs/db412.htm

www.ingramcontent.com/pod-product-compliance
Lightning Source LLC
Chambersburg PA
CBHW071904200326
41519CB00016B/4501